Running an Effective Training Session

Patrick Forsyth
of Touchstone Training and
Consultancy

Gower

First published in hardback 1992 by Gower Publishing

This paperback edition published 1994 by
Gower Publishing
Gower House
Croft Road
Aldershot
Hants GU11 3HR
England

Gower
Old Post Road
Brookfield
Vermont 05036
USA

CIP catalogue records for this book are available from the British Library

ISBN 0 566 07320 X (Hbk)
        0 566 07619 5 (Pbk)

Typeset by Poole Typesetting (Wessex) Limited and printed in Great Britain at the University Press, Cambridge

Contents

List of figures

The author

Patrick Forsyth has spent some 20 years in marketing consultancy and training. Based in London, he is a founder member of Touchstone Training & Consultancy, which specializes in both training and consultancy, and the creation of training materials (including audio and video material).

He has worked in a variety of industries and countries, both in continental Europe and further afield, for instance in South East Asia.

His own training is essentially practical. He runs public courses, working for such organizations as the Institute of Chartered Accountants and other professional bodies, as well as commercial organizations and the City University Business School. He also conducts in-house courses. His organization works primarily in marketing areas, including sales and communications skills, as well as marketing itself.

Mr Forsyth is the author of a number of successful management books, including *Running an Effective Sales Office* (also published by Gower, who also produced two training resources, *20 Activities for Developing Sales Effectiveness* and *Perfect Pitch* – on making competitive presentations). Other publications include *Marketing Professional Services* (Pitman/Financial Times), *The Selling Edge* (Piatkus), and the modestly titled *Everything you need to know about Marketing*, a humorous guide for the non-specialist (Kogan Page).

*"I dunno" Arthur said "I forget
what I was taught. I only
remember what I've learnt."*

Patrick White

*To teach is to
learn twice*

Japanese proverb

Preface

'Well begun is half done'
Proverb

It is not only trainers who train and it is not only courses that are used to convey a training message. Training may involve a full course of several days' duration, but is just as likely to involve short sessions, an hour or two or a self-contained training input within some other, longer, meeting. In both cases the person doing the training may well, for reasons of cost, logistics or involvement, need to be a line manager rather than a 'professional' trainer. This seems to be happening more and more in the current environment.

And yet making sure that training is always effective is important; and it certainly does not just happen. For the line manager (or the less experienced trainer) it can be difficult and time-consuming. My own introduction to training began while I was working in a line management (marketing) position. Looking back, I can clearly remember the first training session that I ever conducted. Let me rephrase that: I will never, ever, forget the first training session that I ever ran. (It was a two-day programme on telephone selling, run twice – Monday/Tuesday and Wednesday/Thursday – each for half the team in a sales office which had to continue operating during the training.) My previous presentational experience consisted of perhaps three sentences, commencing 'Good morning, ladies and gentlemen, may I introduce…', and handing over, with relief, to someone else. Moving from this to two full days was, as I recall, just a little traumatic.

It was not that I had not thought about it, more that either I did not know how to think about it, or that the things which actually needed thinking about did not become apparent to me until I was on my feet. Somehow I got through it. The client seemed well pleased; certainly they booked more work. However, I knew it could have been better.

There is no definitive 'right way' of training. One can spend a lifetime fine-tuning approaches, and from every session you learn something new about the process. What is certain is that I would have benefited from a more systematic briefing before I started. I had attended training sessions, talked to – indeed worked with – trainers, done many things which helped, but despite this I was inadequately prepared.

This book is intended to be what I would have liked at that time. Not that any book could ever provide the complete answer; certainly, this one does not try to. However, it does review, in a practical way, the main issues, and provides guidelines in key areas for all those embarking on an involvement in training whatever their platform for this may be – it is intended to be as useful to line managers as to anyone with, or acquiring, a full-time training responsibility. It presents the fundamental principles in a manageable way that will assist practical implementation, and thus ensure that effective training takes place.

The book has no academic pretensions, and is, as much as anything, a distillation of what I have found and observed works over the years. In any area of business, training can only ever provide knowledge, develop skills, and change attitudes, and often is asked to do all three together. These are not ends in themselves. The overall intention is to improve efficiency, effectiveness and thus results. Time spent on training can, indeed should, be very worthwhile. This book is meant to be a small contribution to making it just that.

Patrick Forsyth
Touchstone Training & Consultancy
17 Clocktower Mews
London N1 7BB

Acknowledgements

'I get by with a little
help from my friends'
John Lennon (with Paul McCartney)

A colleague with whom I used to work tells a story of a course he once ran. One participant was adamantly non-participative, and as the morning went on looked less and less comfortable. Finally, after a number of questions had failed to produce a response from him, the trainer asked bluntly 'Are you with me?' This at last prompted a response, 'I was with you right up to the moment you said "Good morning"' he replied.

Not true, I am sure, but it reminds one of how much in training comes from the participants. Their feedback makes you think about what you are doing, and seek – constantly – for better ways of going about it. So, first, thanks are due to all those who have attended training events of one sort or another which I have run over the years, in whatever organization, country or circumstances. Without their feedback I would be poorer in many ways. Second, to training colleagues over the years who have helped, cajoled or, in some cases, made me run things I thought I never could. Training is simply not a solo activity.

I am also grateful to Maxine Morse, Director of Product Development and Marketing at Longman Training, for permission to adapt and include in Chapter 6 material I originally wrote to accompany one of their training films. And to Stuart McNair, who runs that most useful organization the National Training Index (which provides objective advice to those seeking appropriate training suppliers), and those in Routledge, Cable and Wireless and Minolta, for permission to reproduce their course assessment forms.

For the rest, the responsibility is mine as to whether I have said the wrong thing, or omitted to mention some source, now lost at the end of a chain of revision and adaptation.

PF

1 Introduction

'Change is not made without inconvenience, even from worse to better'
Richard Hooker

What exactly do we mean by training? The simplest definition is surely that training is 'helping people to learn'. But learn what exactly – and how does this learning take place? In industry, commerce, and non-commercial organizations too, training takes a multitude of forms. Some is self-development, the organization is not, or is little, involved, and the people concerned are doing everything from reading a book to attending evening classes. This is not what we are specifically concerned with here, other than noting that it is often in the organization's interest to encourage it. Some firms go further, supporting, advising and financially encouraging such activity.

Here, by training we are discussing the more formal aspects; courses, seminars, 'workshops' – the terminology is ill-defined, and these and a variety of other words describe events with, sometimes marginal, difference of size, length, participation, and so on. We shall keep in mind the typical training event, a short course of perhaps one, two, or three days' duration, and consisting of a number of sessions. We shall review management training, though this also covers a multitude of topics, formats and levels in terms of who is being trained. The typical company trainer may work at a variety of such levels, organizing and conducting training in practical, technical skills linked to either production or administration. They may also work in management, interactive and social skills – communication, supervision, interviewing skills, presentational techniques, the conduct of appraisals, and other skills with more external implications such as selling and negotiation. Some topics for training are desirable, but they have a long-term effect; others are urgent; still others are virtually mandatory (like certain Health and Safety training). The permutations, if not strictly endless, could certainly form an extensive list.

One may wonder why all this training takes place. I have never seen the number of such courses run in the UK (or anywhere else, for that matter) listed; it is probably unknown. Bearing in mind that much training is subcontracted, with consultants, trainers and academics being retained to conduct courses, the fact that the National Training Index* in the UK lists more than 700 organizations offering courses, either as public events or on an in-house basis, gives some idea of the scale of activity. Trainers running programmes for their own organization will add many times to this number, and the overall number of events must be at least tens of thousands per year.

Education is sometimes maligned, but few, if any, dispute that it is desirable. Similarly, for organizations, their success, however they measure it, is dependent on their people. However high-tech, well equipped, or sophisticated an organization is, it is the people who make it work; or prevent it from working as it should. The people and the quality of what they do and how they think and operate, make or break any organization. Further, in today's competitive market, differences in performance – even small differences – affect the results at the end of the day. With some this is obviously so; lack of proper performance in quality control or customer care – it is said that if something is done well for a customer, he or she will mention it to a friend or colleague, but if something goes wrong it will be mentioned to ten (and as I draft this chapter in an airport, where the best current information is showing a 24 hour delay, I for one am inclined to believe it!). In other cases, performance short-falls may be better disguised, or may be long-term in their effect: but they all still matter.

So training is necessary to maintain performance. More important, it is necessary to develop and fine-tune performance with an eye to the future, and to anticipate changes, so they can be better coped with, thus avoiding problems and exploiting opportunities. We live in dynamic and unpredictable times. Large changes come about, sometimes as predicted, sometimes as a complete surprise, and events such as the Gulf War and the UK recession, both in 1991, have a considerable and far reaching impact. Nor should the impact of smaller changes, and the way in which they develop, be underestimated; what did we do before fax; yet it started in a low key way?

It is against this kind of background that training has to operate. It is, or should be, a continuous process, though training budgets can be all too readily slashed in difficult times. It has a part to play, in the sense that it has a variety of input to make, from induction training of new recruits to retirement planning and, sometimes, enforced severance. And everything in between: either in its own right, or as part of the long-term development and succession planning, which is intended to retain the best members of staff and build their competence and potential as they move up through the organization.

So training has a significant role to play. Whoever does the training (and the responsibility is with line management, who are increasingly conducting some of it, not simply specifying and initiating it), it is important. It is linked to change, improvement, and ultimately to the better well being of the organization in terms of whatever the performance factors are by which it may measure itself. Yet

---

*The National Training Index is a subscription service offering a guide to the providers of training, their availability, specialization and quality. They are in London (and may be contacted on 071-287 2172).

training can only have this role if it is successful in two ways: first, it must be credible; second, it must be effective. Each is worth a comment.

The credibility is vital. Although training may be considered as being merely a staff function within an organization, this is no excuse for it being a backwater. Training – and the same applies to the trainer – must create the right image and positioning for itself within the organization. Much can, of course, assist in this; committed senior management for one. It is the trainer who must take some kind of initiative to ensure that this is achieved and the same goes for any manager wanting to do this within his own section. A training department which is well regarded will receive both requests for involvement across a wider spectrum of the organization's sphere of activities, and more consideration for their views and suggestions. Time may need to be spent on achieving this but, as the Bible has it, 'By their deeds ye shall know them'; the ultimate assurance of credibility is to know your subject and provide good training. And that, in turn, means that it must be effective.

What training does, all it can do, can be summed up in three phrases: it can impart knowledge; develop skills; and change attitudes. If it does all of these, in whatever combination (a programme may aim to do all three), and does it in a way that produces positive change, then it can be deemed to be effective. Not only is this going to stand the department or manager in good stead in an immediate sense, but it can build a reputation for excellence which can have an additional impact in the long-term.

So training is a positive part of what makes any organization work; it can be credible, effective, and make a real difference. This relates to the individual as well as the organization. When I began working in training it was quite common to meet participants who had been *sent* on programmes, sent in the sense of ordered to attend. Often this was without explanation of any sort, and a proportion saw the fact as negative, perhaps seeing it as a slur on their performance. Not only did such an attitude mean they tended to obtain little from a programme, at worst their resentment made them a disruptive influence, and the possibility of this occurring, though it cannot be completely ignored today, was a constant factor that made effective training more difficult.

Today, most people who are likely to attend courses have grown up with a more positive attitude towards training. We may bemoan the amount of training done in the UK, viewing it as insufficient or downright inadequate, but even in companies who do comparatively little, what is done may well have a positive effect. Budget limitations certainly prevent many people who would like to undertake more training from doing so. But most people approve of training: they see it as useful, they see it as linked to career development, and they may well see it as making their lives, or at least their job, easier, more interesting, or both.

This shift in attitudes towards training bodes well, and means that trainees are for the most part on the trainer's side – they *want* to obtain something from it. Neither does it hurt if they find it enjoyable. There is no reason why learning cannot be fun, and every reason why being able to do something better as a result should be satisfying.

The next question, of course, is *how* does anyone make sure that the training they give is effective? What is involved in making it successful? Like so much in business life, and in management, there is, sadly, no magic formula. A number of different factors are necessary. It may seem that the first one is an omniscience with regard to the topic of the training. Without any doubt it helps to be well informed, better still well experienced, in whatever it is. However, something that needs to be learned early on in training is that if a question has to be answered by saying 'I don't know', then it can be. The world does not end, the ground does not open up under your feet – perhaps the group of trainees does not actually expect you to know *everything*. (And in any case, there are many ways of handling such a question; perhaps someone else in the group knows; perhaps you can look it up or consult someone else in the next break; perhaps the point has no answer, but needs some debate. We return to this in Chapter 6.) Knowledge of the topic is one of the requirements, however. In addition, the trainer needs to be a good presenter. That much is obvious, yet presentation skills on their own are not enough, people are not expecting entertainment – certainly not only that – rather, they expect enlightenment. To be more specific, they expect to learn: and their bosses may expect it too. So some knowledge of how learning takes place is also necessary.

Yet this is still not sufficient to make a good trainer. A good training session is interactive: people need to be involved, a group needs to be worked, so skills in this area are also necessary. In addition, the trainer needs to be able to structure the session and prepare himself, the materials, and the group. He needs to be familiar with the methodology of training, from simple questioning techniques and discussion to role-playing techniques. He must know about support materials and their use, including resources such as training videos.

Of all these, preparation comes first, and that cannot be done properly until clear objectives have been set. It is to this area that we turn in the next chapter.

2   Establishing a basis

'Knowledge advances by steps, and not by leaps'
Lord Macaulay

Why is training necessary? The answer may seem obvious: surely if one of our employees cannot perform a certain task, or cannot perform it to the required standard, then training is needed to deal with the deficiency. To an extent, of course, this is so, and the same can be said for a group of employees. But real life is more complicated. People have a multiplicity of training requirements, and there are other factors, not least time and cost, that influence whether training can be prescribed in this instant way.

The analysis of training needs is a continual process. It is the responsibility of line management, but the trainer may well have to become involved, or indeed volunteer to participate. It need not be complicated, but it is a process that should take place; and on a regular, ongoing basis. There is a link here with the annual appraisal. Since the advent of legislation whereby, for example, dismissal may be contested unless properly documented, annual appraisals have become more common. That doesn't mean that they are always done well. This can be tested in an organization by simply asking those who receive annual appraisals what they think of them. If they dislike them or find them irrelevant or unhelpful, then you know there is scope for improvement. If the appraisers are also unhappy about them, then there is a serious problem (though it may be one which can be solved by training – showing the appraisers how to do it properly, and appraisees that the process should be constructive). In any case, the process now described parallels that of appraisal. It is made up of a number of stages and, having been through these, the trainer must still set clear objectives. These, in turn, must relate to the jobs that people do, and to how they learn.

The stages are as follows:

- Analyse the job to be done
- Analyse what the job may involve in the future
- Analyse the people
- Set priorities
- Decide the appropriate methods

- Implement the training
- Evaluate

Now let us examine each of the stages in more detail.

Analyse the job to be done

The process starts not with the people, but with the job. In fact this is logical: after all it is quite possible that the process will identify faults which cannot be changed by training. There are only two responses to inadequate performance (other than simply putting up with it, which is not to be recommended, but which does happen). The first is to teach people to do whatever it is better, and ultimately to the required standard; the second is to fire them. Few, if any, of us relish the last option, but realistically there is nothing else to be done, (though 'firing' may shade into such grey options as sideways promotion).

At several stages the questions are the same:

- what are areas of knowledge,
- what are the necessary skills,
- and what attitudes must be evident

for the job to be done satisfactorily? This must first be asked of the job, but in the fast moving world that most businesses inhabit, this is not enough.

Analyse what the job may involve in the future

The same three questions about knowledge, skills and attitudes apply, but the object is to anticipate changes that will affect the job in the future. A simple example will perhaps make this clear. Consider someone in an office, handling customer enquiries. They must know the product, and be able to give a prompt response and good service. They must, from the company's viewpoint, be persuasive, etc. But looking ahead there are other factors. Let us imagine that the department is installing a computerized ordering system. This will impose a completely new series of factors on the basic job as it was, including the ability to work the system and complete the new attendant documentation.

Such a situation clearly adds to the job brief. Often, though not, of course, always as dramatically, this is the case with many jobs at a particular moment. One can also imagine a situation where the changes eventually become too sweeping for people to keep up with. For instance, our customer services person may not actually be able to cope with the technology.

These first two steps will together set out a comprehensive picture of the job; as it is now, and including any anticipated changes.

Analyse the people

The same questions are then asked about those presently doing the job under examination. There could be a gap between what needs to be done to meet an objective analysis of the job, and the current ability of the people to do it satisfactorily. Training is there to close the gap.

(*Note*: all these stages involve *investigation*. On occasions the needs may be clear; more often they need to be sought out or, at the very least, checked.

This may involve observation, literally watching and listening as people do things. It may require discussion with them, either generally or utilizing a check-list or questionnaire style approach; such discussion may be with an individual, or more broadly based. It could involve people around a department, their manager, those in other departments with whom they liaise, people outside the organization – customers or suppliers, for example – and senior management whose policy or strategy sets the basis for how they should operate. Whether this sort of investigation and analysis is brief or more complex, it should always take place, and training should be based on the real situation. It is never likely to be satisfactory to run a course simply because it 'seems like a good idea'.)

Set priorities

It would be wonderful if training could be produced, like a rabbit out of a hat, whenever and wherever needed. Would that life were so simple. It is far more likely that the training plan for any individual employee will have a number of aspects on it to address. They will not be the same in either urgency, complexity or nature. In addition, other factors may be involved: the timing of the instal-lation of the computer system mentioned earlier will no doubt dictate, at least to a degree, the timing of any training given.

So the next step is to list what ideally needs to be done, and then to realistically set priorities.

Decide the appropriate methods

Given the priority training to be done, it is still necessary to work out how it will be conducted. Do a group of people have common needs? Is a course indicated? How long is it likely to take? Does a basis for it exist (or will it have to be originated from scratch)? From which budget will the training come? Where will any course be held? What other logistical and operational problems need to be considered (there are always some, and they may not be easy to solve)? Back to our customer services example. Training may be essential, but fitting it in and keeping a continuous level of service available for customers will doubtless present problems.

Implement the training

Then, as they say, all that has to be done is carry out the training. Preparing and doing that is the subject of the rest of this book.

Evaluate

It may be tempting just to run the course and move smartly on to the next one, but evaluation is important. (This is a separate topic reviewed in Chapter 7).

As was said earlier, in a sense this is a simplistic approach, but the logic is sound. There may well be many circumstances where nothing very much more than an overall evaluation, perhaps with some attendant documentation, is necessary. At the other extreme, there are longer term considerations to the whole process. Succession planning, for example. What is the long-term future of the individual? Is a small training input important in its own right, or as a step towards a longer term aim relating to the progress of an employee through the organizational hierarchy; or both? All of these kinds of consideration may run in parallel.

From this total picture, however, must come manageable training needs. While not ignoring the more complex aspects, many are simply discrete training inputs required on individual topics. Figure 2.1 shows how an individual's training needs form a continuous cycle of development.

Figure 2.1   The continuous cycle of development (from *Running an Effective Sales Office*, p. 134).

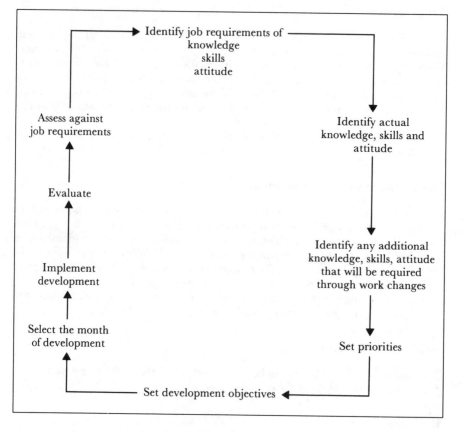

At this point we introduce an example which can then be referred to progressively as we proceed through the remainder of the text.

Example

Making Effective Presentations: The Brief

Let us imagine a review of training needs at a medium sized company, focused on a group of middle managers. All are shown to have one particular weakness. They are poor at formal presentations, one task that is a requirement of their various jobs. So the Training Manager has been asked to recommend ways of staging an event to improve the skills of middle and senior management in formal presentations. Their situation is not unusual. Most do some presentations, but the need to do so is increasing. Some presentations are internal (presenting plans to the Board), some external (to customers, not least). One manager has just become Chairman of a Trade Association committee, and will need to do more rather publicly. Some of them are nervous at the prospect of such a course, but most recognize its potential value and necessity.

Time is (as ever) a problem. We assume that a one-day session is called for, though it will perhaps be repeated (this is to keep the example reasonably simple – a two day programme on this topic, at which each individual can do more is, in many ways, preferable).

The need is clear. The people need to be able to make better presentations.

This theme is picked up as we move on; a perennial topic is chosen so as to avoid a more specialized focus, which is therefore relevant to fewer readers. Presentations is an area that many trainers find they need to include in their portfolio (and of couse, have to do themselves), as well as being a topic with which the author regularly deals.

So far so good. Analysis has shown a clear need. It is a priority, and there is a common group of people involved. Next we set a date and start the training. Or do we? What else needs to be done? Well, consider: 'make better presentations'. Better than what? Better than the worst they have ever done; better than the average of the group, what exactly? While the intention is clear, the detail of what is involved leaves a little to be desired. Which brings us logically to our next sub-section.

Setting training objectives

Business books, advice, maxims – all exhort us to set clear objectives. Sensible advice it is too, and training is no exception. Clear objectives help: they help make sure the right people get the right training, and that it works and is effective.

Having mentioned maxims, let us consider one: objectives should be *SMART*. This is an acronym for Specific
>   Measureable
>   Achieveable
>   Realistic
>   and Timed

(Incidently, acronyms, which have a word spelt out by the initial letters of the words that make them up – as above; and mnemonics, which simply spell out something memorable, though not a real word, both have a role in training – and thus are particularly appropriate here. Back to objectives.)

Saying that training designed to ensure people make 'better presentations' is needed may simply not be sufficiently clear to be useful. If we go back to our example, we can see how the SMART approach applies.

Example

Objectives for a presentation skills course

- *Specific*
  To enable participants to make future presentations in a manner and style which will be seen as appropriate by their respective audiences, and which will enhance the message they put over.

- *Measurable*
  In other words, how will we know this has been achieved? Ultimately, in this case by the results of future presentations; but we might also consider that the trainer or the group, or both, will be able to judge this to a degree at the end of the event by observing the standard during practice.

- *Achievable*
  Can this be done? The answer in this case will depend on the prevailing standard before the course. If the people are inexperienced and their standard of presentation is low, then the answer may be that it cannot. If, as we assume for the sake of our developing example, they are people who are sufficiently senior, experienced and with some practice in the area of presentations, then the objectives should be achievable – given a suitable amount of time and a suitable programme.

- *Realistic*
  Picking up the last point, if the time, say, is inadequate, then the objectives may not be realistic. These people can potentially be improved we might say, but not in one short session.

- *Timed*
  Timed in training terms will reflect the timing of the course; it may be scheduled to take place in one month's time, so the objectives cannot, by definition, be realized before then. Also the duration: is a one, two or any other number of day programme going to do the job?

If you can always develop training objectives in this way they are likely to be much more useful than the briefer objectives. It could also be that more effective training will come from them than would be the case with a less precise set of objectives.

Having considered this, preparations can begin – presently. Before preparing anything you have to consider other aspects, in particular the basic principles of how people learn.

What makes people learn?

There are a number of factors which are regarded as making it more likely that people will learn, and learn more easily than might otherwise be the case, from any kind of communication. Some of these are examined later (for example, the use of visual aids is discussed in Chapter 4). There are four main principles, however, which it is useful to consider early on, and certainly before preparing a particular session: effect; forward association; belonging; and repetition.

Effect

People will more readily accept a message if it is positioned as something that will affect them, and which will preferably do so positively. So, for example, a new system is better described not just as being more efficient and a measure that will save the company money, but rather as making the operator's task more straightforward, and which will also, because it improves customer service, give a more positive feedback from outside the company (and is more efficient and saves the company money).

To use this principle to the full necessitates the use of empathy, that is the ability to see things from the other person's point of view. In any case, this is a valuable asset for anyone in training. Of course, careful phrasing to make sure that something is put this way round is likely to improve the impact it makes in training terms. This works in two ways: first, by ensuring that people quickly tune in on the message – 'this is for me'; and second, by influencing their longer term acceptance and consideration of what they are having put to them. This is really only common sense; it may have been researched and categorized as learning theory, but it simply boils down to the age old principle of 'what's in it for me?'

Forward association

This principle is concerned with sequence. People tend to remember things in the order in which they are communicated, learned or subsequently used (if you doubt this, try saying, for example, your car registration number backwards. Because that is not the normal way, because it has been learned and is used the other way round, most of us find it slower to recite it backwards). This has implications for a clear sequence and structure or, better still, a clear structure and sequence. For instance, if we say there are three key factors about . . . subject X then there should be three, well chosen factors: we should not spend the next half hour saying '. . . and another thing I should have mentioned is . . .'.

More of this when we review preparation in the following chapter.

Belonging

People relate more easily to the things of which they have prior personal experience or knowledge. If this is not the case, with discussion perhaps entering areas where it is new territory, more scene setting will be necessary. Imagine trying to teach someone to drive if they had never sat in a car before, and compare this with the learner who has been brought up in a family owning, and using, a car.

Such a consideration reinforces the idea of knowing something about the group, specifically or in general terms; it helps to know something of what their prior experience includes. Where this is not possible, or where information is minimal, seeking feedback even as the session proceeds is helpful in influencing how it should be conducted. The old saying about information being power is as true in training as anywhere else.

Repetition

All the statistics tell us that people forget very easily; half of everything you tell them will be gone within a week, so it is probably no surprise that repetition is an aid to learning. This does not mean, necessarily, verbatim repetition. Though there is a role for this – to put over a clear, precise, definition perhaps. Repetition more normally means approaching a subject in another way, explaining by analogy or example to repeat a point in a different way for emphasis, for example.

In other words, if you go over things a couple of times, in different ways, then people . . . but you get the idea.

All of these are basic points; it pays to bear them in mind because they crop up in a variety of contexts throughout the training process. All will help people to learn, making it more likely that the message will 'stick', that more will be remembered, and thus that the changes that we seek in behaviour, performance, and so on will come to pass.

In addition, if the group are finding it easier to understand the topic and its detail, they are likely to find it more satisfying, and their attention will be kept that much more easily. This is part of the process of achieving one accolade that most trainers appreciate, that is simply when someone says 'I understand'; better still the whole group.

Two of these factors are worth linking. Effect and belonging are a formal part of what makes training relevant to the participant's job. This is important. The relevance of a message to an individual will not necessarily be seen unless it is spelt out. If this is not done, then much of the time spent in seeking for any relevance may become a distraction to members of the group. It cannot be spelt out too clearly how training fits in with what the *trainees* do, or will do. While there is a role for training which is less technique-based, less how-to or job related, this needs to be set up very carefully, and those perhaps longer term or more attitude-oriented objectives spelling out very carefully.

One final principle is a logical part of this view, one which is again only commonsense, but is nonetheless useful for that.

Training sequence

Training sequence relates to the overall sequence of putting across any message, and can be highlighted by a series of questions.

Why is the training taking place?   This puts the training in the broadest context, and links it to the main issues. Perhaps the organization is expanding (or as this is being written in a time of recession, contracting); perhaps changes are afoot, such as reorganization. People see the relevance of any sort of training far better if it is related to the main context in which it takes place.

What is the specific relevance of any task?   The individual aspects of the training need to be put in context. Launching into, say, a dissertation on regression analysis techniques may make sense, but equally it may confuse. Regression what? It is always worth placing every detail in context.

What exactly is the task?   The task may seem obvious, but it too needs spelling out. This can be done in a number of different ways; by description, by example, by demonstration – but it must be clear.

How is it done?   This is the detailed explanation. It may be three sentences or three days worth, depending on the complexities of what is being taught.

How do I do it?   This stage is not always catered for directly, but basically involves practice, and with some skills the opportunity to experiment. It must be made clear that practice does not automatically imply the need to turn in a perfect performance. Exercises and other devices may provide a kind of alternative to real practice; they are protected, and play a part in this stage.

How am I doing?   This question implies feedback. Practice is doubly useful if it highlights progress to date and lets people see whether anything has been learnt. There is also an element of support inherent at this stage; in other words, advice and assistance is progressively available.

Will you leave me alone?   Participants now need to actually do the activity, to do it unsupervised, on their own. This is the final test, and training may well have given them a heightened consciousness of what they are doing, and a greater ability than before to fine-tune their own performance. Indeed, this is a very valuable by-product of training – one that it is worth seeking to include amongst its effects.

Now what?   On-going training will provide on-going feedback. There is no sharp line between learning and doing; people come back, there is further checking, supervision, and monitoring; and the whole process continues.

To some extent the above is somewhat idealized, but the principles are right. It may not always be possible to take as long over training as you would wish, to explain as thoroughly, or practise as extensively as if time and money were no object. However, there is a minimum amount in these directions that will give what is necessary; ultimately, only experience of the process will allow you to judge what is appropriate.

Finally, considering all this, we return to the earlier example.

Example

The group we considered earlier need presentation skills training. They need the following explained:

- Changes in circumstances inside and outside the organization make more, more formal presentations necessary.
- What kind of presentations? These need defining in terms of length, type and purpose.
- What is depending on them? It must be spelt out that plans will not be confirmed, customers will not be persuaded, etc., unless the presentations are right.
- Standards need spelling out. Do they have to be as good as people in another division, in the competition – and how do we judge if they are good enough (perhaps simply by the plans *being* approved)?
- Details of the course content: spell out what it will cover.
- Identification of practice sessions (with people using their own, relevant, examples).
- And perhaps this can be linked to the next real presentation each course member will have to do, which might be observed to create more feedback and opportunity for further improvement.

Such is not the only way in which this explanation can be thought through, nor does it necessarily give a comprehensive view of the coming course. It does, however, illustrate how an approach of this sort sets the scene for any programme, and makes it more likely to run smoothly.

To an extent, much of this is background, but practical background, and all the principles referred to in this chapter make a difference to the session that will be conducted. Individually the points made are straightforward and commonsense; together they show why training – good training at least – does not just happen; these commonsense points need orchestrating if the whole is to work well.

Even with all this, a good training session is rarely delivered 'off the top of the head': it needs preparation. That is the topic we move on to in the following chapter.

3 Planning the session

'The human brain starts working the moment you are born and never stops until you stand up to speak in public'
Sir George Jessel

There is an old story of the manager who pledged to find a one-armed management trainer. He was asked why. 'Just to have someone who doesn't say "on the one hand this . . . and on the other hand that . . ." he replied. So: consider presentations. On the one hand, training presentations should be straightforward. After all, they are for the most part factually based. There is a body of knowledge to put across and, if you know your topic, you should be on strong ground. Further, for the most part people like training. The culture of any good organization will encourage it, and see that it becomes associated with progress, greater personal interest and improvement. Indeed, ensuring that this is so may well be part of your job.

But – there is so often a but – on the other hand, as the quotation which began this chapter makes clear, there are difficulties. It is not like chatting to someone over a desk. There are expectations; there are risks, and you are, inevitably to a certain extent, exposed. There are, however, ways in which to build on the first aspect and to tackle the second in a manner that will create a satisfactory whole. This chapter sets out to review both.

An earlier chapter mentioned preparation in the sense of putting the programme, plus individual sessions and all their components, together. This chapter considers preparation in detail before we move on to execution. Preparation is the key to successful presentation. Do not doubt it, underestimate it, or skimp it; you will do so at your peril. A good speaker can range far and wide from his plan, but (with rare exception) he will have thought about it and, while the degree of preparation will of course vary, that it should always take place is a fundamental rule.

HOW TO PREPARE

Assuming you already have a clear programme outline, we concentrate here on preparing the presentational elements of a session. This starts with consideration of the group, and the individual members of it. In training the numbers are normally manageable, with perhaps 8–15 people being best, with a few more on some occasions. This may not be as daunting as a massed group of, say, 400 in a conference centre, but you may well have to cope with large numbers, at anything from departmental meetings or sales conferences to gatherings of the whole company. In any case, every size of group presents a different challenge. Whoever they are, and however many of them there are, you need to think about how they will feel about the training.

It helps to have clear answers to a number of questions as preparation is started:

- who are those in the group?
- do you know them?
- do they know each other?
- how long have they been with the organization?
- what job function and level of seniority do they have?
- what previous training have they had?
- what will be their expectations of, and attitude to, the training (it may also be useful to ask the same of their manager(s))?

Such considerations may consist of anything from simply a few moments' thought, to some checking, to the circulation of some kind of pre-course questionnaire. You can't ever know too much about the group. Besides, it avoids surprises, some of which may result in a need for adjustment to the plan so that you are able to cope with them (a fact that will be vouched for by many). Those who have been faced with an all woman group, for example, after planning for a mixed-sex group – or as happened to me, a group where half the participants could not speak English, will confirm the need for adjustment to the training plan. The most bizarre case I have ever heard of was a presenter who, having prepared his input around a veritable pile of overhead projector slides, realized that 80% of the group in question were blind!

Before turning to the detail of what preparation entails, it is appropriate to mention one very important factor; your *lecturing notes*. This may seem like running ahead, but as preparation leads up to the point where, with the right kind of *aide memoir* in front of you, you start the session, it will make better sense to consider your lecturing notes as we proceed.

While the detail individuals need will vary, practically everyone needs some notes. The newcomer to training should certainly not attempt to work without some clear guidelines in front of them. But what exactly is appropriate? One aspect that needs to be worked out is the style of notes that suits you. It can be in any style you like, but it must be practical. For instance:

- A loose-leaf ring binder may be best, ensuring that material stays open and flat in front of you (a binder with pockets in the front and/or rear covers allows you to store 'exhibits' that go with the course material – a brochure perhaps – conveniently in the same binder).
- A4 pages may be better than cards (which some like, and which may suit a lectern) as you can see a reasonable amount of what is ahead at any one time. This also allows some kinds of overhead projector slides to be put in the same binder.

- Writing/typing on one side of the paper allows additional material to be added, or amendments made easily.
- Use a suitable size of words, or type. This affects how you use the notes. I find, as a spectacle wearer, that when standing I can read normal typed material best from a binder placed on top of a briefcase (or something of a similar size) laid flat on a table, rather than on the table itself.
- If using an A4 page, a good bold line dividing it into two or three segments, or enclosing a section in a box, will give the eye several smaller areas on which to progressively focus, and make it easier to keep track of how far you have gone as you proceed.
- Always number the pages; there may well be quite a lot of material. Some like to number in reverse order, say with page 40 at the front and thus page 1 at the end. This helps to estimate the time remaining (you may well come to be able to estimate how long a typical page of your style of guiding notes takes you to work through), and still acts to keep things in order.

Such notes are *not* in any sense a script. Reading material *verbatim* has little or no place in training. There are some short exceptions, like a definition or technicality that may need to be quoted precisely. Reading can not only sound dull, but it can be difficult to do (try reading part of this page out loud without stumbling). Extemporizing from good notes is easier, and will give a better effect. While everyone needs to find – by experiment, no doubt – what suits them, an example may serve as a model, and to prompt thinking. Simple symbols can be used to save space, and act as a more obvious prompt than simply a word:

Ⓢ   – indicates when to show an *overhead projector slide* (if you sometimes use 35mm slides you may prefer OHP).

Ex   – indicates when there is *delegate* participation (and can expand on how, as in 'working in pairs': Ex(× 2)).

?   – specific *questions* asked of the group.

E.g.   – *examples* of what is being discussed.

Op   – used as a prefix to the others when there is something *optional* (when time permits).

You may want to evolve others for a variety of points:

- summarize on flipchart;
- hand out materials;
- introduce/show film/video;
- tell anecdote;

and so on. Figure 3.1 gives examples.

Now, it is not suggested, at least not to begin with, that preparation starts with a blank sheet of paper and ends with a complete documented session in one simple step. So how does one go about it? What produces good training, yet does not take forever? It needs a logical process which moves through several stages.

Figure 3.1   Symbols for lecture notes

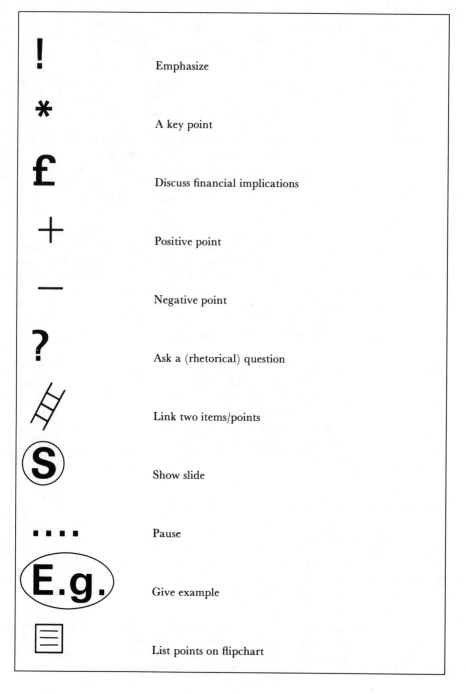

Building it up

Training programmes do not, for the most part, spring into being tried, tested and raring to go, with notes, slides and everything required to hand. (The possible exception is published training materials of the kind described in the appendix.) To put them together successfully, the planning process seems to work best when travelling from the general to the particular; in other words, designing an outline and then filling in the details.

Let us review an example through several stages to see how it takes shape. This book is intended to be useful to managers and trainers wanting to train in the widest range of subjects. My own background is in sales and marketing, which is perhaps too specialized to provide a good example. So the chosen topic is formal presentational skills, already touched on in Chapter 2 and developed now in more detail. This, while it overlaps with selling – many presentations have to be persuasive – is a general skill, and one very necessary to a wide range of people in many kinds of organization (see the example on p. 9 for the presentational skills brief).

If someone who has never previously delivered training on this topic was to start from scratch, what would they need to do? We review and illustrate this process in six stages:

1. *Listing:* all the points to be involved, from what needs to be said and done, to timetable and ideal delegate number.
2. *Sorting:* editing, arranging and sequencing the list of contents and components.
3. *Arranging:* producing a complete 'game plan' for the training, including timing.
4. *Method:* deciding exactly how the training will be delivered and taken, i.e. what *both* trainer and delegates will do.
   (*Note:* (3) and (4) may have to be considered together, as method can influence timing.)
5. *Materials:* specifying all materials (permanent and usable) for both trainer and delegates, including noting sources of, for example, training videos or equipment which may need to be hired.
6. *Reviewing:* checking that the plan is complete and that all its components fit.

There is still preparation to be done following this before the training can be organized and conducted, but the basis for the event will be created by this approach. The stages, which overlap to some extent, are now taken in turn.

Listing

This is a technique (sometimes called 'mind mapping') for writing a document, especially a particularly complex one. It starts by ignoring the sequence, or a least the detail of it, and not worrying about structure, simply listing everything regarding the programme as it comes to mind (it is how the chapters in this book were first put together). Mind mapping is illustrated in Figures 3.3 and 3.4.

Figure 3.2 shows what might initially be produced for the presentations session. It may not do so at a single sitting, of course, but as it takes substance, one thought will lead to another. Conversely, when the mind grinds to a halt it doesn't matter where the next starting point, is or what is put down next. In fact, this initial process is better done 'freestyle' than as a list. Figure 3.3 shows how this begins to make more sense.

Figure 3.2   Preparing the programme: listing

Making effective presentations

Introduction
Visual aids
Preparation
Structure
OHP – using it
Dangers/pitfalls
Use of humour
Presence
Mannerisms
Initial impact
Making it clear
Ending on a high note
etc.

The obvious way of putting down the course elements is to write a list. It works better, however, to put points down more at random; the links and logic following more easily – as in Figure 3.3.

Sorting

Sorting simply rearranges what you have listed more logically, while still ignoring the fine detail of structure and sequence. Note that some of the questions raised may need to be answered before it is possible to move on to the next stage. For example, how many attend the training session may have a direct effect on the timetable, the quantity of participation possible, and so on. The presentations example is shown in this revised form in Figure 3.4.

Arranging

This stage adds the timing, and lays out the whole programme in a structured form. Figure 3.5 continues the presentations example. There can clearly be an overlap with the next stage here, or even the next two stages, depending on the topic. Stages (1) to (3) comprise what is sometimes called 'mind mapping'.

Figure 3.3 Preparing the programme: listing with the 'freestyle' approach

Preparation – what to say
– how to say it

Introduction (by example)

Presence
eye contact

Visual Aids ⟨ OHP
flipchart

Handouts
"Props"

Structure – Beginning – initial impact
– attention/rapport

– Middle – developing the argument/clarity
maintain interest

– End – on a high note

Participation – individual introductions
and presentation

Voice – pace
– emphasis

Critique – lessons
checklist

Timing (judging it)

Dos & Don'ts

Fielding questions

Use of humour

**A snapshot of how this picture builds up, allowing some structure to begin
to develop. The next figure shows how the basic list can be annotated.**

Figure 3.4   Preparing the programme: sorting

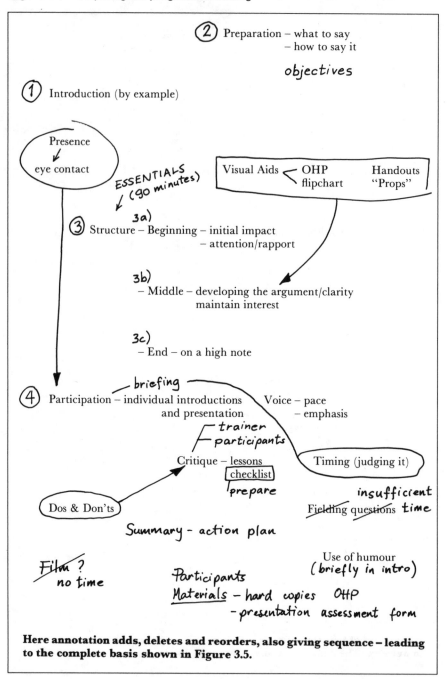

Here annotation adds, deletes and reorders, also giving sequence – leading
to the complete basis shown in Figure 3.5.

Figure 3.5   Preparing the programme: arranging

Making effective presentations	

Making effective presentations

9.00–9.40
1. *Introduction* – overview of key elements
     – Examples; e.g.: opening
        use of question
        dramatic pause
        humour
        visual (slide)
        end on high note
     – individual introductions

9.40–11.00
2. *The Essentials of Presentational Technique*
     – preparation/ objectives
     – structure
     – notes
     – stages (beginning/ middle/end)

11.00–11.15   **Break**

11.15–11.30
3. *Introduction to Individual Presentations*
     – the presentations
     – the equipment
     – analysis
     – the details

11.30– 1.00
4. *Presentations*
     – presentation
     – analysis
     – discussion

1.00– 2.00   **Lunch break**

continued

Figure 3.5   Preparing the programme: arranging – *concluded*

2.00–5.00
5. *Presentations (continued)*
   Note: 30 minutes per presentation
   will allow two in the morning (the
   first always taking longer) and six
   in the afternoon – a group of
   eight.
 	
5.00–5.30
6. *Summary* and close	

Method

Because of the effect a method has on the trainer, his preparation, the delegates, and on learning, it is worth considering separately, (see Figure 3.6).

Figure 3.6   Preparing the programme: method

Making effective presentations	

9.00–9.40
1. *Introduction* – overview of key
   elements
   – Examples; e.g.:
   opening
   use of question
   dramatic pause
   humour
   visual (slide)
   end on high note
   – individual
   introductions
	Method
	Lecture
	   – structured to *show*
	   examples (10 minutes).
	Discussion – led by question: 'What
	   was demonstrated? (or
	   omitted?)'
	
	Individual input
	   – 2 minutes each (max).

9.40–11.00
2. *The Essentials of Presentational*
   Technique
   – preparation/
   objectives
   – structure
   – notes
   – stages (beginning/
   middle/end)
	Lecture
	   – with some question/
	   discussion

11.00–11.15 **Break**	

Figure 3.6 Preparing the programme: method – *concluded*

11.15–11.30
3. *Introduction to Individual Presentations*
        – the presentations
        – the equipment
        – analysis
        – the details
	Lecture
	        – and question opportunity
	        to ensure clear
	        understanding

11.30– 1.00
4. *Presentations*
        – presentation
        – analysis
        – discussion
	Individual inputs
	        – filmed/critiqued against
	        trainers checklist of
	        'points to raise' (the
	        details)

1.00– 2.00 **Lunch break**	

2.00–5.00
5. *Presentations (continued)*
    Note: 30 minutes per presentation
    will allow two in the morning (the
    first always taking longer) and six
    in the afternoon – a group of
    eight.
	Individual inputs
	        – filmed/critiqued against
	        trainers checklist of
	        'points to raise' (the
	        details)

5.00–5.30
6. *Summary* and close
	Lecture
	        – final questions
	        – individual action plans

Materials

Here decisions are made on what will be used, by whom, why, and to what effect. Actually preparing them, making slides or writing notes, comes later. Fashions change in this area (and attitudes vary in different organizations and in different countries). Some favour extensive materials, some minimal notes; different topics will also need different back up. What materials are necessary 'on the day' should certainly be considered: papers, exhibits in front of the group during the session; and what resumé material is necessary to form a source of reference after the course?

The former includes a variety of items, from a graph that is too complex to make into a slide but which everyone must look at together, to an exercise sheet with only a handful of words on it, but which is to be completed during the session. With resumé notes, the current feeling, (at least in the UK) seems to have swung towards something shorter rather than longer, though whether this is because a book-style resumé is unnecessary, unused, or simply expensive and time consuming to produce is a mute point.

Again, the illustration in Figure 3.7 shows this stage.

Figure 3.7 Preparing the programme: method/materials

Making effective presentations	
9.00–9.40 1. *Introduction* – overview of key elements – Examples; e.g.: opening use of question dramatic pause humour visual (slide) end on high note – individual introductions	**Method** *Lecture* – structured to *show* examples (10 minutes). *Discussion* – led by question: 'What was demonstrated? (or omitted?)' *Individual input* – 2 minutes each (max).
9.40–11.00 2. *The Essentials of Presentational Technique* – preparation/ objectives – structure – notes – stages (beginning/ middle/end)	*Lecture* – with some question/ discussion. Distribute – hard copies of OHP slides used.
11.00–11.15 **Break**	
11.15–11.30 3. *Introduction to Individual Presentations* – the presentations – the equipment – analysis – the details	*Lecture* – and question opportunity to ensure clear understanding Distribute – presentation assessment form.
11.30– 1.00 4. *Presentations* – presentation – analysis – discussion	*Individual inputs* – filmed/critiqued against trainers checklist of 'points to raise' (the details).

Figure 3.7 Preparing the programme: method/materials – *concluded*

1.00– 2.00 **Lunch break**	

2.00–5.00
5.   *Presentations (continued)*
     Note: 30 minutes per presentation will allow two in the morning (the first always taking longer) and six in the afternoon – a group of eight.
	Individual inputs
	        – filmed/critiqued against trainers checklist of 'points to raise' (the details)
	
	Distribute
	        – resumé notes.

5.00–5.30
6.   *Summary* and close
	Lecture
	        – final questions
	        – individual action plans
	
	Distribute
	        – personal action plans.

Figures 3.1–3.7 show how the trainer would document these stages. A 'published synopsis' will also be needed, and this may be more like that shown in Figure 3.8.

Figure 3.8 Making effective presentations: synopsis

Making effective presentations

A fast, effective way for middle/senior management to improve a valuable skill.

Objectives.   This one-day session sets out to review the process of making an effective presentation, showing how to:

● understand and work with a group
● plan and prepare
● present more effectively
     and build confidence and technique.

Coverage

Introduction.   The essentials of a good presentation – what makes it work – the dangers – an overview of the techniques: **Discussion and Personal Introductions.**

continued

Figure 3.8 Making effective presentations: synopsis – *concluded*

The Essentials of Presentational Technique.   Objectives, preparation, a logical structure and preparing notes – the stages of the presentation:

- The Beginning – gaining attention – creating impact – building conviction/rapport.
- The Middle – presenting and explaining individual points – the importance of clarity – maintaining interest and conviction.
- The End – techniques for summarizing – obtaining agreement/commitment – ending on a high note.

The Details. Using visual aids – manner and mannerisms – emphasis, pace and timing – 'props'. **Presentations** – each participant will make a short presentation*; this will be recorded on video, played back and used both as an opportunity to see how each participant performs, and to provide a basis for **discussion** of details that help or hinder the process.

Summary.   Action for the future.

---

*The **Briefing Note** attached gives details of this.

Note: Figures 3.2–3.8, building up the one day presentations course, are intended as an example of the process rather than a model of how to conduct this kind of programme (though it is a realistic method and would work perfectly well, there are other ways of going about it).

Similarly, the methods suggested suit the example, and do not form a comprehensive list of what could be included – everything from people working in pairs or on a case, to training videos, audio tapes and other examples; whatever is appropriate to the topic of a particular course.

Reviewing

This is the final check; a review of shape, structure, sequence, timing. Everything that might affect the preparation of trainer and materials. It is wasteful to spend hours working out an exercise for a programme and then find it takes too long, and will not fit the allocated time.

Once you have gone through this thinking stage, final preparations can follow. The detail in putting together your lecture notes which you need in front of you is the next issue.

The format of speaker's notes

To give an example of the sort of notes you may have in front of you during your presentation, we return to the presentations course example. What follows is by way of an example: it is not suggested that this is the only, or necessarily the best way in which to begin such a session (though in the right circumstances, notes along these lines work well): nor is it suggested that the format of notes should be followed slavishly. However, it does allow the principles being applied to be illustrated. Ultimately, what matters is that the individual finds the notes both comfortable and in a practical format with which to work.

First, the introductory section is set out *verbatim* (though it is difficult to describe the full effect of a presentation in print). Then the notes from which this might have been presented are shown (Figure 3.9). In real life this is best done in (at least) two colours. To complete the picture, the first introductory slide is shown in Figure 3.10, and then the checklist, Figure 3.11, shows how some of the factors included in the introduction to illustrate presentation in action can be used in discussion. This introduction is used to lead into an early discussion session, with the objective of involving everyone, and quickly addressing interesting aspects of the topic.

Linking back to the text on the preparation of such a programme, and studying the sequence from there, is intended to illustrate an encapsulation of training in action.

Now we turn to the sequence referred to above, and start with the *verbatim* text of the introductory minutes of the presentations skills session.

What was actually said

[People have assembled for the session. Informal discussion has no doubt been taking place, and we join the session as the clock hits 9am and the trainer makes a formal start.]

"Right. Let's make a start. Thank you for all being in good time, we have a busy day ahead. As you know, the topic is 'Making effective presentations', and the session is predominantly participative.

Briefly, first we'll run over a few administrative points, then I shall set the scene and we'll discuss that and see where we go from there. At that stage too, as not everyone knows each other, we'll go round the room and give everyone the opportunity to introduce themselves.

So, admin first . . . [here the trainer runs over a few points, ranging perhaps from when notes will be distributed to where the loos are located] . . .

Now to the topic of the day. You all make presentations, and do so for a variety of different reasons. There is a common factor here that affects everyone. This can be illustrated by communications you receive; maybe a letter from a customer or an internal memo from a director. There are some which, though they start ever so politely. . . 'We were grateful for your presentation', then continue . . 'but . . .'. And the net result is no order; no agreement; no go ahead for the plans you presented, or whatever.

We all know the feeling. And after all we did. But why? Afterwards we start asking questions about what happened; about the presentation:

● was it too long, or too short?
● did they not understand it, particularly if it was technical?
● did you inadvertently pick your nose, or pick holes in a member of the group?

Figure 3.9 Lecturer's notes

	Making effective presentations
Intro:	time/participation
— admin	— timing — notes — questions (link to training plan) — breaks/lunch — messages

Set the scene	The topic of the day — presentations
	
	                            different reasons/
	                            common importance
	
	          common factor — a lot hanging on them
	
	            internal memo --> no agreement
	                    to plans
	
	Inquest: despite effort — what happened?
	
	      ?long/short
	      ?technical
	      + holes/nose
	
	Not 100% ... but 'if only...'
	
	        'The human brain is a wonderful
	        thing — it starts working the
	        day you are born — goes on and
	        on, and only stops on the day
	        you have to speak in public.'
	
	Improvement — more preparation
	               — minor/major problems
	
	   afterwards too late — no second chance/
	            prize

Today: review the structure/techniques
        process:

        and practice — TV
                    'real life examples'
                    discussion
                    — no problem
                    (details to come)

Emphasis: — make it easier
          — certain/effective
          — fun

                    (questions)

→   discussion

                    (see checklist)

        — what went on (and did not)
          over the last few minutes?

                            example?

At that stage you will never know for certain, but sometimes we know there were problems and we begin to say 'If only . . .', 'I shouldn't have . . .' to ourselves. We do know it could have been better and, worse, we often feel that if it has been a simple one-to-one meeting rather than a presentation, it would have been better.

You may know the old saying: 'The human brain is a wonderful thing – it starts working on the day you are born – goes on and on, and only stops on the day you have to speak in public'. (The original version appears at the start of this chapter).

Often, making it better only needed some more preparation beforehand. Occasionally what went wrong is less clear, or there may be more serious omissions. Afterwards it is certainly too late . . . there is usually no second chance, and no second prize.

Today, we shall do two things – review the process of presentation, and practise it.

To be specific, we'll review the structure of a presentation, and the techniques that make for an effective one.

And practice . . . that's you on TV. Sounds a bit traumatic. By the end of the day you'll hate yourself, your colleagues, and especially me! Not really. Actually, while it does give you an opportunity to see how you perform, it is more important in providing real life examples of the sort of things that crop up for us all to discuss. I think you will find it useful. More of this later. I'll make quite clear how it will all work before we have to do it.

The emphasis on both the review and the practice is deliberate. It is designed to help:

- make presenting easier;
- make it more certain and effective;
- even to make it more fun.

Now, are there any questions at this point, before we move on?"

Figure 3.10   Slide used in the presentation's introduction (designed to be shown in three stages)

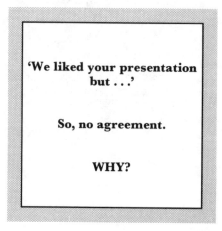

'We liked your presentation
but . . .'

So, no agreement.

WHY?

Figure 3.11 Presentation checklist

After the pause at the end of the introductory session there may be questions from the group. Once these have been dealt with appropriately, the trainer can again take the initiative.

A discussion at this point will involve everybody, will air further the issues that will be dealt with during the day, will put people more at ease (video work *is* somewhat worrying), and will begin to ease people into the topic.

Such a process can be started with a question . . . 'Think about what I have just done in that introductory few moments; can we list any techniques that were involved – and indeed, any that were not, and perhaps should have been?'

Then points can be listed (and perhaps a few words said about each. These might include:

- giving a clear brief (was it?)
- early link to the specific jobs of those in the group
- an early, rhetorical, question (Why?)
- use of a quote
- a little humour
- a dramatic pause
- putting people at ease, or at least starting to, about the video
- a lead into a discussion and participation
- an opportunity to ask questions
- use of visual

Similarly, what was *not* done or used? For example:

- no handout (yet)
- no-one addressed by name

and so on, and so on.

Again, none of this is the only way of proceeding, but it helps complete a comprehensive example of this part of the proceedings.

There is one final element you may want to include and, while you must not overdo it, it is worth a slight digression.

Humour in training

Humour is a serious business (and a sensitive one, sorry about that). This is true of humour in general, and of humour in training. Now things said out loud in a meeting or in the pub which are hilarious may not solicit anything like the same reaction when read off the page. There is an important point to be made here, however, so I will press on (as sensitively as possible) to try to review this, briefly, in print.

It would be a dull training course that did not raise a few laughs. Some will come through the normal interaction of any group. Some may need to be prompted by the trainer, who is, after all, responsible for the whole well being of the group over a few hours or days. And some humour can make a point, and contribute positively to the learning, which is why the subject is worth a mention here.

The problem about humour in training is that it is largely unpredictable, and for the trainer who cracks a joke that falls flat, the ground opens up as deep as for the failed comedian. Do this regularly and the trainer risks not being taken seriously. (Now that may have been what he intended; for a moment, but not in that way). Humour can be useful, however, and occurs in three main ways:

- *informally*: in the breaks, say, or as an aside that arises, unplanned, in the discussion. This does no harm, and in fact a less serious moment in the breaks may bring the group back to work with their concentration restored. A trainer may like to have something planned for such moments, but must resist the temptation to be a comedian if manifestly he is not. Remember, it needs more than a good story to make it work; it is also 'the way you tell them!'

The other two are planned, first:

- *intended humour*: which does not really break the continuity of the course, but is intended to inject a momentary relaxation, or even make a point. This really comes in two varieties. The first is well illustrated by the quotation at the start of this chapter ('The human brain starts working the moment you are born and never stops until you stand up to speak in public'). No-one is going to laugh uproariously at it, nor is its use intended to have that effect. Nor even, and this is important, is anyone likely to feel that it was so intended. It is the sort of thing that should prompt a wry smile, even from those that have previously heard it. And that is the intention of such remarks. Furthermore, on a training session relating to presentation skills it is not a million miles from the topic. Such humour is safer than a joke and, in passing, quoting is safer than other types of quip; if it is not funny you can blame it on whoever said it originally. It is worth keeping an eye (ear?) open for them, especially those that link to topics you deal with regularly.

It is perhaps invidious to try to illustrate this with examples, certainly extensively; humour can date so quickly, and the publishers assure me they will sell this book for years to come. However, a couple I came across recently make the point. One genuine quote:

- The late Isaac Asimov, the well known and prolific science fiction writer, is reported to have been asked what he would do if he was told he had only six months to live. He replied in two words 'Type faster'. (One day that will fit in with something on writing skills.)

And one anecdotal quote:

- Did you hear about the manager who received a memo from the Training Department nominating him for a course on delegation? He wrote back saying he could not make it – but would send his assistant. (After all, he was so senior he had people to delegate *for* him). Two quips together can reinforce what is done.

The second type is:

- *a real, and longer, joke, story or anecdote:* more care is needed here – try them out on a colleague or the family rather than just the bathroom mirror, to be safe. Again, a real link with the topic is welcome. If the laugh is not quite what is hoped for the link still stands. There are not so many with a good point and appropriate link, but again they are worth looking out for and adapting and embellishing as necessary. They can make good 'ice-breakers', perhaps leading in to a new topic.

One I used successfully, having heard it just prior to acting as a guest speaker at a company event, went as follows:

- A new, smart, top of the range Volvo estate car, boot full of expensive riding gear, tow bar, driven by a smart rather 'county', clearly rich lady driver is making a total mess of parking in the only space in the car park. As it moves back from the spot for the 27th time a flashy sporting saloon, the kind with built-in bumptiousness and a driver to match, nips through the gap into the vacant place. The driver gets out, and, as he locks the door, shouts to the lady driver 'That's what you can do if you can drive properly'.

  Without a pause she reverses back, hard, into the side of the car door, the tow bar accentuating the impact. In the silence after the sickening crash she winds down the window and calls over 'And that, young man, is what you can do if you have money'.

In the time it takes for a book to appear you may well have heard it, but it got a good laugh and led neatly into the topic of the better utilization of company resources (the first of which to be reviewed was finance). If you like it, leave it a year to two before you use it; everyone will have forgotten it by then. Mind you – unless this book sells beyond the wildest dreams of either author or publisher, in which case it will have had too much of an airing – I will too. We can start it on its rounds again together.

Humour must not be inappropriate, and must not be overdone; but omit it completely, and your training may become like verbal Mogadon.

Incidentally, did you hear the one about the Training Manager who . . .?; but I digress; let us return to the next, more serious, topic.

The whole process above works well and seems more likely to create a good programme than the, seemingly, logical alternative of simply constructing everything on one sheet of paper in chronological order. With a good sound basis set out first, the personal preparation of the trainer prior to course delivery is always more straightforward. Indeed, a well thought out programme will work better for trainer and participants alike.

4 Preparing course materials

'The shortest pencil outlives the longest memory'
Proverb

Any training session is an event. It is an experience for those who attend (and for the trainer for that matter). What participants take away is an amalgam of everything that has happened. It blends elements including what they heard, saw and did, and can involve other senses. What did they touch – in an equipment demonstration, perhaps? What did they taste – it could just be lunch or the product launch of a new food product? So they take away impressions, some of which will last; others need, and may receive, progressive reinforcements; some will, inevitably, be rapidly forgotten, as was touched upon when the way in which people learn was discussed.

They also take away, or experience, or use, materials. There are a variety of these, and they fall into a number of distinct categories. Some of these are for the trainer, some for the participants, some for both. Let us take those for the trainer first.

TRAINER MATERIALS

Perhaps the most important items are the 'lecture notes' – the guiding documentation the trainer plans to have in front of him during the session to act as a kind of 'route map'. They set out the structure, content and method. Whatever they look like – and the only real criterion is that they suit *you* – their preparation was dealt with in some detail in Chapter 3.

Second, the trainer needs a set of those materials the participants will have issued to them. Third, a number of other things are needed, e.g.:

- equipment
- exhibits
- the 'trainers guide' for a (rented) video
- visual aids
- props.

Some of these are commented upon below.

Visual aids

Visual aids are very important. Remember that one of the factors mentioned in Chapter 2 was the power of a visual image rather than an aural image.

The first category are those aids that are used to add a simple message to the proceedings. These have two different advantages:

- *for the trainer* they can act as an additional progressive guide to the structure and content of the session, as with the way one would work down a stack of overhead projector (OHP) slides. Incidentally, many types of OHP are framed in a way that allows reminder notes to be written to the side (in a way, of course, that remains hidden from participants when the slide is shown, but which is visible to the trainer). *Note:* visual aids are a *support* to the session. The tail should not wag the dog, they are there to reinforce, exemplify and illustrate what is being presented or discussed. They must not take over. A presentation which has no slides may be dull in comparison with one which does. On the other hand, one that uses too many, particularly checklist-style slides (i.e. predominantly words), may become over-structured around their use in a way which is also dull or becomes too predictable.
- *For the group* they represent a proven aid to learning and, no less important, some variety. In addition, they may provide other effects, including humour. (By way of example, Figure 4.1a presents a simple but powerful image designed to emphasize the importance of listening. Figure 4.1b is a classic optical illusion showing how sensory information can be interpreted in sharply differing ways.)

In summary, visual aids can:

- present a great deal of information quickly
- improve the understanding of a presentation
- give visible structure to the verbal communication
- *allow a visualization* of the main thrust of an argument, and 'position' the message before it is examined in detail.

The most common forms of visual aid are:

- flipcharts
- OHPs
- table top presenters
- fixed whiteboards
- handouts.

Figure 4.1. (a) Ears cartoon. (b) Beauty and the Beast (Source: Picture Collection, The Branch Libraries, The New York Public Library).

The advantages and disadvantages of such visual displays can be compared as follows:

Flipcharts

Advantages	*Disadvantages*
– no power source needed	– expensive to prepare
– can be prepared beforehand	professionally
– can be adapted on the spot	– very large and cumbersome to
– easy to see	carry to an outside venue
– usually available in some form	– masking is difficult and can be
– easy to write on	untidy
– colour can be used	– can sometimes look messy
– you can refer back to earlier	– may not stand up to constant use.
sheets.	

In general, flipcharts are more useful as a group 'work pad' than as the basis of a presentation.

Overhead projectors

Advantages	*Disadvantages*
– can be seen in even a bright room	– need a power source
– produce a large image	– can be noisy
– masking is easily possible	– projection lens can block the view
– prepared slides easily carried	of the screen
– can look professional	– can break down
– commonly available	– limit to amount of information
– can be used sitting down	that can be legibly projected
– aide-memoire notes can be	– require a screen or a suitable wall
written on slide frame	– tidy use requires discipline and
	experience*
with acetate roll attached:	
– can also be used as a group work-	– not easy to write on without
pad.	practice*
	– OHPs providing an acetate roll
	facility are usually bulky
	machines, though modern 'flat'
	OHPs are available with an
	acetate roll built in.

OHPs are generally best used as the prepared base of a presentation, while the acetate roll is more useful as a 'work pad'.

---

*See page 43.

Table-top presenters

Advantages	*Disadvantages*
– all the advantages of a flipchart	– can look too 'flashy' to some
– easier to prepare professionally	groups
– easily carried and 'put up' in a	– masking is not easy
training room	– require skill to ensure they
– can be used when seated	remain only an *aid*
– more informal, yet professional	– only work with small numbers.

Generally, table-top presenters are an effective compromise, allowing pages to be prepared in advance and 'work-pad' notes to be made. They also facilitate alterations.

Fixed white boards

Advantages	*Disadvantages*
– increasingly available in training	– need special pens
rooms, etc.	– not easy to write on
– useful for 'work-pad' noting to	– limited space
aid group discussion	– usually require erasing of writing
– often metal backed, allowing	before additional comments can
prepared papers to be displayed	be displayed.
with magnetic disks.	

Useful only as a 'work-pad' on which to highlight a few key points.

Handouts

Advantages	*Disadvantages*
– can portray our professionalism	– usually not personalized
– highlighting of relevant points is	– parts of content can be irrelevant
possible	or even counter-productive
– can convey our technical	– can detract from our verbal
expertise and give third party	presentation.
references.	

Generally useful as a support for the presentation argument, but it is not easy to condition and control the perception of the aid itself.

Increasingly, other aids – 35mm slides, video tapes, computer displays – are entering the presentational arena. Most can be excellent in their place. Most also distance the audience from the presenter. The most successful presenters will therefore use them with caution, since they know the final impact will be dependent upon the participants' acceptance of the credibility of the trainer and the message, not on the supporting elements.

Figure 4.2 sets out the general principles for the preparation of visual aids and, to focus on perhaps the most used and most useful, the box opposite it reviews in detail how to use an OHP effectively.

Figure 4.2   General principles of preparing visual aids

- Keep the content simple
- Restrict the number of words:
  - use single words to give structure, headings, or short statements
  - do not cause the aid to look cluttered and complicated
  - personalize with firm's name or logo where possible (or course title)
- Use diagrams, graphs, etc., where possible to present figures. Never read figures alone without visual support
- Build in a variety within the overall common theme:
  - use colour
  - build in variations of the forms of aids used
- Emphasize the theme and the structure:
  - continually use one of the aids as the recurring reminder of the objective and agenda (e.g. prepared flipchart)
  - make logical use of the aids (e.g. OHP for base of presentation, flipchart or whiteboard for highlighting comment)
- Ensure the content of the visual matches the words:
  - make the content relevant
- Ensure the visuals can be seen:
  - are they clear?
  - what are the room limitations?
  - what are the equipment limitations?
  - use strong colour
  - beware of normal type-face reproduced on slides unless enlarged
- Ensure the layout emphasizes the meaning the aid should convey.

Finally, in what is an important area, the main rules in using visual aids are:

- Talk to the group, not the visuals.
- Use colour to highlight key points.
- Talk to the group while writing on a visual aid.
- Avoid impeding the group's view of visual aids.
- Explain graphs and figures or any complex chart.
- Remove an aid immediately when it is not longer required.
- Tell the participants what they will receive as copies. It is often useful to issue slides in hard copy after the session.

Using an OHP

Some care should be taken in using overhead projectors to begin with; they appear deceptively simple, but present inherent hazards to the unwary. The following hints may be useful:

- make sure the electric flex is out of the way (or taped to the floor); falling over it will improve neither training nor dignity.
- make sure you have a spare bulb (and know how to change it) – though many machines contain a spare you can switch over to automatically – test both.
- make sure it is positioned as you want; for example, on a stand or a table on which there is room for notes, etc. Left-handed people will want it placed differently from right-handed people.
- stand back and to the side of it; it is easy to obscure the view of the screen.
- having made sure that the picture is in focus, look primarily at the machine and not at the screen; the machine's prime advantage is to keep you facing the front.
- only use slides that have big enough typefaces or images and, if you plan to write on acetate, check that the size of your handwriting is appropriate.
- switch off while changing slides, otherwise the group see a jumbled image as one is removed and replaced by another.
- if you want to project the image on a slide progressively you can cover the bottom part of the image with a sheet of paper (use paper that is not too thick and you will be able to see the image through it, although the covered portion will not project).
- for handwritten use, an acetate roll, rather than sheets, fitted running from the back of the machine to the front will minimalize the amount of acetate used (it is expensive!).
- remember that when something new is shown, all attention goes, at least momentarily, to the slide; as concentration on what you are saying will be less, stop talking until this moment has passed.
- it may be useful to add emphasis by highlighting certain things on slides as you go through them; if you slip the slide *under* a sheet or roll of acetate you can do so without marking the slide.
- similarly, two slides shown together can add information (this may be done with overlays attached to the slide and folded across); alternatively, the second slide may have minimal information on it, with such things as a course title, session heading or company logo remaining in view through the whole, or part of, the session. This is illustrated in Figure 4.3. Alternatively, masters can be used to provide various standard backgrounds to which other words or images can be added (see Figure 4.4).

If you want to point something out, this is most eaily done by laying a small pointer (or pencil) on the projector. Extending pointers are (in my view) almost impossible to use without looking pretentious, and they risk you having to look over your shoulder.

Figure 4.3   Two slides with one background image

Slide

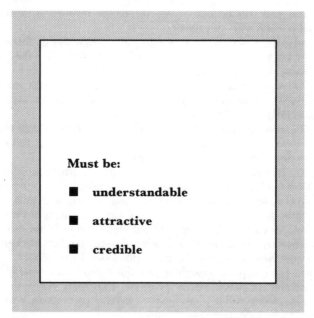

Overlay

Figure 4.4   Example of standard background slide (ideally using a second colour)

EQUIPMENT/EXHIBITS

I once worked with an American consultant who ran an excellent seminar on pricing stratgegy. If such a seminar was done in a hotel meeting room he always ordered two hard-boiled eggs with his breakfast, one brown, one white, along with a raw onion. He received some funny looks, but used both as exhibits, props if you prefer; the first to illustrate customers' fickle attitude to price (people will pay more for brown eggs than white), and the onion to make a point about market segments. So, as this clearly illustrates, the materials a trainer might need at a session are many and various.

It is an area for which you may usefully evolve a personal checklist. Some of the items on this will be straightforward. For instance, you may list equipment you use regularly, and having mentioned equipment, an obvious but often overlooked point is worth stressing: *always, always check all the equipment before the session begins*; not only before, but far enough ahead to have time to rectify any problem. At a recent meeting I ran for a group of hotel personnel, having stressed the need for them to do this for those hiring their meeting rooms, I switched on the projector. It lit up; I had checked that it would. But the acetate roll, which I had *not* checked, was jammed and would not wind on. I now check that as well!

Checklist

Overhead projector   – spare bulbs
                      – acetate roll
                      – pens
35mm slide projector
Flipchart   – spare paper
Whiteboard
Pens for flipchart/whiteboard (*note:* whiteboards need special pens which will not leave permanent marks)

Other

For delegates   *Misc*
Notepaper   Aspirin
Pens/pencils
Other stationery (e.g. rubbers, pencil sharpeners)
Name badges (for lapels and table cards)
Calculator

And of course all their notes, binders and documentation. You may well add more and create a personal list.

Exhibits may include such items as the eggs mentioned earlier, but as well as anything to which you may need to refer, you may also require various other objects to hand, either to show, to make a point with, or to issue to all participants. These will include obvious items like company or product literature or product samples, and can also include a range of other items, e.g.:

- Photographs
- Plans
- Posters
- Advertising material
- Items relating to competitors
- Systems, forms

A further element often brought into course sessions is the video training film. This is valuable, yet must be used carefully – it is worth another short digression.

Using training films

The days when the only available training films were American have long gone. For many years a number of producers have been steadily increasing the amount of home grown material, and much of it is both extremely professional and extremely useful.

Too often the film, more usually, of course, in video form these days, is regarded as an entity in its own right. A good film may well teach lessons of itself, but they are nearly always more powerful as an integrated part of a session or course. If their use is planned in this way you will achieve more by using them. But we are running ahead of ourselves. The first job – often by no means straightforward – is to select a film to use.

Film quality does vary. Some films have a well defined purpose, and will not suit any and every group. The first source of films is the catalogues, though it's worth saying immediately that no trainer should ever use a film that they have not viewed in its entirety before the session. The questions the trainer should ask come back to having clear objectives for the session:

- what is the point that needs to be made to the group?
- is a film an appropriate way of doing it (or part of it)?
- what attitude changes are involved in the process? Would a film help with this?
- is the style of the film (the settings and situation) compatible with our organization? If not, can inferences still be drawn from it?

In part, the decision will be influenced by how the film will be used. Will it, for instance, be a curtain raiser; something to spark discussion, lead into role play or summarize? And how will the film fill this role? Some thought here is always sensible, and it is rather too common to find a film being included just because 'there should be a film'.

There is certainly more to showing a film than simply saying 'Now we will look at a film' and pressing the switch. Tina Tietjen of Video Arts, who knows a thing or two about training films, set out in *Managing Sales and Marketing Training*, a Gower handbook which I edited, an approach to using films which is worth quoting here:

Assuming a film is to be used as part of a fuller training session, the film presenter should do certain preparatory work:

1 View the film completely.
2 Make notes on the following:
   (a) significant scenes which relate to his training message and his organization.
   (b) significant phrases and expressions used by the characters which typify employees in his organization.
   (c) any training points picked out or captioned in the film.
   (d) any 'below the line' training points in the film. These will be points not captioned or mentioned in the dialogue but dropped in for the sharp-eyed trainer to notice. Memorable examples of these have been:
   – the clock in the interviewer's eyeline in the Video Arts selection interviewing film 'Man Hunt'.
   – the incorrect placing of telephones on the desk during the John Cleese scenes in the Video Arts film 'Will You Answer True?'
   (e) a series of prompts:
   'What happened when the customer said, "They're too expensive"?' or 'What happened when Sheila said she wouldn't co-operate with the new procedures?'

(f) names of the characters, their job titles and relative status.

(g) points where the film can be stopped to allow for discussion or role-plays to take place.

3 Read the accompanying discussion leader's guide for ideas on how to use the film.

4 Read any other booklets supplied with the film. Such booklets usually extend the lessons in the film and cover related subjects which may not have been able to be addressed in the film.

5 See the film through again.

Having completed this basic preparation the trainer is in a position to plan the training session and decide the role the film will play within the wider programme.

All of this, like so much that makes training work, is in the area of preparation. Beyond this, the use will be influenced by the nature of the particular film. There are two main types:

Case studies   enact a drama, often one involving a series of mistakes, and they typically end with either a series of flashbacks highlighting what went wrong and hence the learning points made, a final scene in which the right way forward is spelt out by one of the characters, or a combination of the two.

Such films make good openers (one example many know is the Rank – now Longman – training film *Who killed the sale?*) They allow the scene to be set quickly, and thus the subject to be broached quickly. In addition, they can highlight mistakes, problems or difficult areas without the necessity for examples from within the organization being quoted, and the subsequent awkwardness this can sometimes create. They provide a common framework for discussion, and often lend themselves to reshowing, clip by clip, so that more detailed discussion can be prompted.

Such a film may well be best shown in two parts, stopping it before the final scene explains everything to prompt discussion, and then running the last section later. This allows key questions to be posed:

- how did the situation come about?
- who was at fault?
- how could it have been prevented?
- what are the lessons for the future?

and so on, depending on the topic.

Right/Wrong way films   usually start with the wrong way and divide the topic into a number of segments. This type of film may again lend itself to being viewed section by section – with participants discussing what went wrong and why, and reviewing possible better approaches before going on to view the next section. On occasions there is no reason why showing a film should not be spread out over a long period, with the gaps in viewing involving exercises and even role playing. The film can always be shown a second time later on to give the satisfaction of continuous viewing.

Similar approaches can, of course, be applied to the 'right way' section, with discussion reviewing lessons and, perhaps, action and systems change that should result. Even the right way may be bettered in some organizations; it is the approach that is most important, not a slavish following of some, after all, fictitious, procedure.

Films provide a different set of memories, different that is from what is said, discussed or dealt with in other ways. Humour has become a popular way of creating memorable images. Some of the Video Arts films are now called, in conversation, the 'John Cleese films' as a result, though he is not in them all. Extreme humour runs the danger of obscuring the message, but different producers favour different degrees and styles of humour; as do users and course delegates. If you use films regularly, it may be worth planning the use of different styles from different producers to ensure they continue to add freshness to the sessions on which they are used, and so that people do not come to expect a similar, 'statutory' film every half day or so. As someone once remarked about a particular trainer, "you can always predict his session, there is one film for every three yards of training."

That said, films are undeniably useful. They vary the pace, add another element, create additional memories, and can be used to lead into constructive discussion, exercises and role play of all kinds. As long as they are seen as a support to the session, with a specific part to play, rather than as an end in themselves or an opportunity for the trainer to have a rest, they can contribute – and contribute powerfully. Make them accelerate learning and they can be a regular part of the training you do, an element participants look forward to, and from which they benefit.

If delegates find that a film is not a 'soft option', but leads into a part of the session that is hard work, then the film is being used wisely.

PARTICIPANT MATERIALS

Participants cannot simply sit and listen. They need to participate (we come to the detail of this in Chapter 6), and they need to remember. The materials issued to participants serve both purposes. There is a role for résumé notes, something to remind them of the course content later and a need for working papers, items the group needs in front of them during the session, to complete exercises and make notes.

Participants' notes are for the participants. An obvious statement, but there can be problems with documents which are designed to be *both* the résumé notes and the trainer's main reference. There is no reason why the two should be so similar. It is also worth noting at the outset that:

- notes can be distributed before, at the start of, during or after a session (or some of each, progressively filling a loose-leaf binder). Remember, people have an irresistible urge to read ahead, so material distributed in advance should not be virtually a *verbatim* equivalent of what you plan to say.
- résumé notes need not, in any case, follow what you say slavishly. It may be better to approach topics in another way (in part this creates learning by repetition).

- hard copies of slides may form a useful part of the participants' notes.
- people best remember things they have heard, seen *and noted*, so notes should be designed to be written on where appropriate.
- the total 'pack' that is finally retained should be of reasonable quality (so they want to keep it), practical (e.g. loose-leaf and able to lie flat), and *personalized*. The latter is important. If the material finally contains the participant's notes, indication of emphasis, action points and so on, it will be more likely to be both retained and used.
- time and cost are involved. A mammoth book style handout will take longer, and therefore cost more, to produce (and to print). A compromise between factors is often necessary here.
- in addition, what is best is also a function of style and fashion. Some organizations favour more or less material; more to be comprehensive, less to make it manageable (some will measure an external training consultant's value by the weight of the handouts they supply, not, it must be said, an infallible guide).

Again, as with so much training, a typical handout 'pack' does not constitute a recommendation for everything, but many events work well with:

- some pre-course reading (this may be background, and might not even be originated by the trainer, e.g. an article).
- some material, predominantly exercises and key points, distributed early in the session.
- résumé notes, to act as a permanent reference, distributed at the end.

The next question relates to format. What should the handouts look like? How should they be designed? So much more is possible with modern word processing (and desk top publishing), and the handouts will be valued far more if they look professional. More important is how they work.

Figures 4.5 – 4.9 contain examples, with comment, of several styles and approaches. The permutations are almost endless, and these may help you decide what is right for you – you may want a 'house-style'. Alternatively, different topics and sessions may necessitate a different approach. The notes-styles text of Figure 4.5, for instance, is perhaps a good example of the kind of 'weight' of text that works best.

Materials people will keep and use

Because it can be time consuming, preparation of materials can easily be skimped, and they may be less useful as a result. Most material is, to a degree, transient: it can be amended, updated and improved, and may change regularly over the months ahead. (Not being able to do this is what makes producing a book so time consuming; most trainers are reluctant to let a book go to print knowing that it cannot be altered for some time.)

Figure 4.5 Participants' material: example of a simple, text-style résumé handout

- Emphasize areas of agreement
- Emphasize benefits
- Meet and overcome objections
  - use examples and stories
  - provide a guarantee
  - make a 'special deal'... a discount, or promotion, etc.
  - provide proof... documents, figures, tests, reports
  - have your customer consult a 'neutral' expert
  - get additional 'qualified' opinions
- Ask for the sale

Be sure that your tools for meeting objections are organized and accessible. Rehearse examples or stories. Have neat attractive copies of any evidence you may want to provide readily available. Have the straight facts about any deals you are able to offer. You are the expert. You are responsible for helping the customer make the best decision. Lead the way.

Price

As a rule, do not sell price — sell value. Sell service, guarantees, value, convenience, and quality.

- Do not sell price — sell value.
- Sell service, guarantees.
- Sell convenience and quality.
- Sell benefits.

- Talk price only when you are authorized to make a concession on price.
- Talk price when 'low-price' is a main product benefit.

STEP SEVEN: CLOSING THE SALE

Attempt to close many times every sale. Convey a confident attitude to the customer — expect him to buy.

Figure 4.6   Participants' material: example of more elaborately produced résumé notes (from a Gower video manual co-written with David Senton entitled *Perfect Pitch*)

2.2   THE STRUCTURE OF A WRITTEN PROPOSAL

Contents

The basic items in a typical written proposal will be:

a) Covering letter
b) Title page
c) Table of contents
d) The body of the proposal
   - introduction: background to the client's requirements and contact with our company
   - our understanding of the client's requirements
   - the terms of reference
   - our proposed solution
   - our competence and staffing proposals
   - time plan for implementing the solution
   - cost justification regarding fee levels
   - summary/conclusion
e) Appendices of relevant information, e.g.
   - profiles of proposed staff who will work on the account
   - procedural and technical details
   - other aspects of our company which it might be useful for the client to know
   - contractual terms

a)   Covering letter

This is a selling tool, not just a letter of transmittal. Therefore, keep it short, usually no more than one page. In a letter:

- announce the submission of the proposal
- emphasize that the proposal represents the mutual conclusion of discussion between ourselves and the (prospective) client
- thank the members for their time and effort in briefing us and for the opportunity to propose working with them
- suggest a timetable and action plan for closing the sale
- write to a particular person(s) and have the letter signed by a partner/ director

and bind the letter into the proposal, if appropriate.

Note: A written proposal should have a covering letter even if it is to be handed to the client during a presentation.

b)   Title page

List:

- the title that identifies the work
- for whom it is prepared
- who is submitting the proposal

Researching and Preparing our Proposed Solution   39

Figure 4.7 Participants' material: example of a checklist approach which is both a summary and is designed to be simply completed

VIDEO CHECKLIST 1

Each part of the video raises issues which may need review to ensure our current approaches are fully satisfactory. The following is intended to highlight those issues in a way that will help to prompt action where necessary.

	Yes	Action
Have we identified, and responded to, market changes creating or effecting the need for competitive presentations?		
Is the immediate handling of incoming enquiries – on the phone – in writing, satisfactory?		
Does such handling immediately begin the process of discovering exactly who the enquirer is and what is wanted?		
Are we clear as to how that response is progressed in terms of – where a meeting takes place? who attends?		
Do we have enough information as we embark on the briefing meeting?		

Have we prepared adequately, particularly
  – our opening?
  – the questions we will ask?
  – how we will describe/position ourselves and our organization and our track record?		

Do we always look the part?		
Do we ask for and retain enough supporting information, literature, samples, etc?		
Do we monitor client reaction throughout the meeting?		
Do we check on competition?		

Do we ask about the proposal
  – when it is wanted?
  – in what quantity?
  – how it relates to any subsequent meeting?		

Do we take adequate notes?		
Do we leave with enough information to proceed to the next stage?		
Have we made a good initial impression?		

Taking the Brief   21

Figure 4.8   Participants' material: example of a simple exercise page, leaving space
to do the exercise work specified

Exercise 6 — Getting through to the right person

Add to the call plan you have prepared a note of any anticipated problem in getting
through and how to cope with it:

Problem   Solution

_____   _____

_____   _____

_____   _____

_____   _____

_____   _____

_____   _____

_____   _____

_____   _____

_____   _____

_____   _____

_____   _____

_____   _____

_____   _____

_____   _____

_____   _____

_____   _____

_____   _____

So it is worth some time and care; a number of points will assist in ensuring it is right. Participants notes must:

- be attractive – well produced material (and this need not be elaborately or expensively done) gets more attention paid to it;
- be relevant – and explain why it is; in other words, it needs constantly to link to the job in hand, improvements to be made, and so on;
- relate to prior knowledge – taking people forward in comfortable steps from where they are at present;
- present information in 'chunks' – in other words, there should be no sections relying on page upon page of solid text; it needs to be structured, with divisions, headings; anything to split it down into bite sized segments;
- be logical – a step-by-step approach works best, adding details progressively;
- be memorable – reflecting and linking to the session and the way in which it was presented, and real life examples and real life cases help here;
- use the laws of learning – with a little repetition, prompting with questions, etc.;

and can contain *options*, digressions adding to the material of the session, with an exercise or project, perhaps.

Also, of course, any material should meet certain practical criteria. It should:

- be logical – obvious, but sometimes items such as representations of slides can present difficulties;
- lie flat – ring binders seem best (which also allows material to be added in future);
- have space – sufficient for notes, annotations and examples to be added without making the whole effect messy;
- be 'findable' – consider a table of contents, dividers, numbered pages, colour-codes (or paper), a glossary, further reading list, etc.;
- be illustrated – where explanation can never be sufficient on its own, slides being reproduced, diagrams, flow charts, even pictures can add considerably to its usefulness.

Finally, the wording – the language – should be appropriate. So some dos and don'ts may be useful:

- Be precise, specific, and make sure that where language is aimed at clear explanation it provides just that (e.g. beware of phrases such as '24 service' – what exactly does it mean, or words like 'soon' – how soon is soon?).
- Use the active voice, in other words, say 'use the active voice', not 'the active voice should be used'.
- Be conversational. Use the word 'You', people are more likely to learn if it is phrased for them.
- Be positive rather than negative (i.e. most of your don'ts are better as dos).
- Explain reasons. Do not say 'You should ask questions', say 'If you ask the right questions, in the right way, the information you obtain will make it easier to . . .'.

Figure 4.9 Participants' material: example of combined résumé notes and note taking facility

3.2 PRICING POLICIES

There are four basic approaches to pricing:

- Cost-based pricing
- Market demand-based pricing
- Competition-based pricing
- Market-based pricing

It is well worth determining price levels in a way that combines all four approaches.

Cost-based pricing (accountants' approach)

This is the approach similar to the way an accountant would calculate the price for a product. It is based on total cost of product, including production and marketing costs, plus an allocation for overheads, plus the target percentage to provide a profit margin. The total gives a selling price.

Problems

- Cost calculation is based on a predetermined level of demand and production. As these fluctuate, so does the product cost.
- It ignores market factors such as demand and competitors' actions.
- Overhead cost allocation can lead to a wrong pricing decision.

A major benefit of this approach is that it can help indicate minimum price levels.

Your notes	Session checklist
	Consider what different prices each approach leads to for one selected product:
	£

Figure 4.10   Specimen memorandum requesting presence on a training course

---

MEMORANDUM

15 December

From: Anthony Patrick — Training Manager
To: Susan Barnet

Subject   Making Effective Presentations
           Training session: briefing

As you will know from the last Departmental Heads' meeting, you are
one of those listed to attend this session. It is scheduled for the
quiet time after Christmas, and will be held on Tuesday 7 January. A
good start to the new year!

This note sets the scene and has with it:

- a synopsis of the content of the day
- administrative details
- a map to help you find the venue easily
- a list of your fellow participants

Why this session? Because presentations are a vital skill, one that
more of the company's managers are having to deploy, and deploy more
often. Many do so well. But much is dependent on many presentations.
Orders. Approval of plans. They have to go just right.

What will it cover? The session will cover two aspects. First, it
will set out the principles involved; second, it will give you an
opportunity to practise and review, with your colleagues, what makes
for a good presentation, and how key issues important to our business
are best handled. And, yes, we will be recording some of it on video
— but I am sure you will find you quickly become used to that, and
that it is a very useful experience.

How will it benefit you? You will receive: an increased awareness of
the importance of presentations — more knowledge about what makes for
a good presentation — it is also intended that you will, at the end
of the day, have not only a better basis on which to prepare and
undertake your next presentation, but that you will be able to prepare more certainly to make the impact you want. In a sentence: we
want to simplify, structure and strengthen the whole process.

Note: You need to come prepared to make a ten minute presentation.
Pick something you know — preferably something you will have to do in
the future (this can act as a rehearsal). As one of the points we will
be talking about is visual aids I am asking everyone to plan to use at

continued

Figure 4.10 Specimen memorandum requesting presence on a training course – *concluded*

least four flipcharts – the sheets can be had from the Training Department, and then they will clip straight onto the stand on the day.

If there is any more information you would like just let me know.

Note:
- Remembering the checklist, for such a course the administrative notes should mention dress; and some would recommend noting on the participants' list in which order the presentations will be done (to prevent people worrying – or worry whoever is first even more?), and mentioning that people will also be asked to introduce themselves to the group.
- Here the tone decided upon is friendly, constructive, designed to begin to put people at ease. This aspect must be matched to the event and the people in question.
- The *synopsis* should probably be circulated in about the detail referred to in Chapter 3 on page 27.

- Use humour carefully (see Chapter 3 on preparation).
- Avoid stereotypes: all the people in stories, cases and examples should not be men (or women). Be careful of age, and minority, groups – though one has to be realistic, and descriptive; for instance, Chairperson is clear and well used, while salesperson does not have as specific a meaning as salesman (one meaning anyone involved in selling in whatever way, the other usually meaning the field salesperson, or representative).
- Watch out for over-use of cliché and stock phrases.
- Do explain abbreviations, at least the first time (e.g. overhead projector [OHP]).
- Do check exact meanings, especially in multinational organizations, simple matters can cause confusion (e.g. if we 'table something at a meeting', in America this means we will not discuss it; in the UK it means that we will).
- If, like me, you are a poor speller, use a machine with a spell-check programme, or ask someone suitable to look through the material and correct it.

There is another item amongst the material (documentation might be better word in this case) and that is the notification that must go to particpants *before* the session. This is an area that seems to suffer from lack of thought. As one who has arrived at client companies to conduct a programme and found myself facing a group of people whose briefing has consisted of little more than 'Be there; at 9am', I know it is important.

The thought required, and the time it takes, are not prohibitive, and a session is likely to go very much better if people not only know what it is about and why they are there, but are committed to its success. The checklist below, and specimen invitation to attend in Figure 4.10 (based again on the presentations example), show how this can be simply, yet comprehensively, done.

Checklist: Pre-course notification

Make sure a note goes to every participant announcing the training event and briefing them as to its nature. (*Note:* remember that the note may instruct, suggest or attempt to persuade people to attend. It may go from the trainer or a line manager, or both – there is good sense in 'the boss' being seen to be involved.)

In every case, make sure that it states:

- what the topic is;
- why it is being scheduled (and why now?);
- what specific objectives are set;
- what benefit they will receive from it (personally) in their jobs, perhaps as specifically as what they will be able to do after attending that they could not do, or could not do so well, before;
- what participation will be expected;
- any preparation that is necessary (and follow up that must be fitted in);
- anything they should bring (from the obvious, something to write with, to the less obvious, a calculator, diary, files, literature, projects);
- who else is attending?
- who is conducting the session?

and any administrative points:

- when is it?
- where is it (and how to find your way there, if necessary)?
- timings;

and anything else considered relevant:

- how will messages be handled?
- how should participants dress? (for our chosen example, where they will be making a presentation, formal 'office wear' is no doubt appropriate; on some sessions an opportunity to be less formal than usual can be taken);
- 'house rules' (e.g. smoking or non-smoking in training room?);
- expenses (if relevant);
- meal requests (vegetarians?);
- an acknowledgement (or even a thank you) if arrangements cut into private time – perhaps they have to travel to the training centre or venue on a Sunday night to start early on Monday morning.

As well as the kind of briefing shown in Figure 4.10, further advice (instruction?) can be given to delegates as an initial part of documentation on the day.

Some years ago I was involved in the promotion of seminars conducted by visiting overseas lecturers and consultants. One regular visitor, an American consultant, gave me a list of 'rules for delegates' which – while designed for public seminars – contained good advice. In anglicized form I have used it in a variety of contexts since, and a version of it is shown in Figure 4.11. Feel free to adapt it further, or use it as the basis for a document suitable for your own organization.

Figure 4.11   Rules for participants

NOTES FOR DELEGATES

1. This manual contains all the basic details of this training programme. Further papers will be distributed during the course so that a complete record will be available by the last session.

2. This is *your* seminar, and represents a chance to say what you think – so please do say it. Everyone will learn from your comments and the discussion which follows.

3. *Exchange of experience* is as valuable as the formal lectures – please *listen* to what others say and try to understand their point of view.

4. In discussion *support your views with facts*, examples or comparisons and stick to the point.

5. *Keep questions and comments brief* – do not monopolize the proceedings, but let others have a say so that several views are made known.

6. Make points as they arise, but remember that *participation is an attitude*. It includes listening as well as speaking. However, never be afraid to disagree in a constructive way, as issues arise.

7. *Makes notes as the meeting progresses*. There is notepaper in the binder for this. It can be useful to note separately three key ideas from each session that you can implement without delay.
    This manual can remain as a permanent record, but only you can make sure that ideas are implemented and the catalytic effect of this programme is not lost.

8. *A meeting with colleagues or staff* on your return to your company can be valuable and ensure information or instructions can be passed on promptly with a view to action.

9. It will be helpful to everyone present if you will

    (a)   *wear your lapel badge* throughout the seminar
    (b)   *adhere to the timetable* so that no time is wasted.

10. Please *be sceptical* about your own operations as well as of the course. Only by questioning present standards can progress be achieved.

Finally, if all this sounds like hard work, and as there is no point in 're-inventing the wheel', as they say, the appendix on pages 113–125 sets out information about, and an example of, the ready-to-use training material now available. Though such material will not always be applicable, much of it is designed to be amended and personalized, rather than followed line by line; it can often be time saving, cost-effective and a practical option.

5 Running the session: Presentational techniques

'Take care of the sense, and the sounds will take care of themselves'
Lewis Carroll

The last chapter made clear the importance of preparation. This cannot be over-emphasized, and I offer no apologies for starting this chapter with the same thought.

First consider the way in which a message is taken in. Comprehension is not a straightforward process, many aspects combine to make it more difficult than it might otherwise seem. Surely, if you know your subject there should be no great problem? This is not the case. Difficulties are inherent, and stem in the main from five areas:

How people hear Or rather, how they sometimes do not hear. People find it difficult to concentrate for long periods, their minds flit about (as yours is doing, perhaps, reading this). This means that messages must be delivered in a way that keeps demanding attention. In addition, people make assumptions about the importance of what they hear. They will reject some points, or 'tune out' for a moment if it does not clearly appear to be an important or interesting part of the message.

How people understand Understanding is always diluted:

- if matters are not spelt out clearly or are confused with jargon. Jargon is professional shorthand, useful when everyone knows it to the same degree, confusing if not – and important because it becomes a habit, one that can take a conscious effort to avoid when necessary;
- because people misunderstand more easily what they hear, but do not see; hence the importance of visual aids;
- because people draw conclusions ahead of the completion of the message, because the sense appears clear to them;
- and because people make assumptions based on past experience: 'Ah, that's like so and so' they say to themselves, when in fact it is not, or proves not to be as the full message is spelt out.

How people change their views   Training often involves asking people to change their viewpoint, often a long held one. This creates suspicion, the same feeling that we sometimes recognize when we deal with someone with 'something to sell'. Additionally, people dislike being proved wrong, and the acceptance of a new view may imply a past mistake in believing something else. Thus the communication has to be just right to overcome this factor.

How people decide to act   Change, of course, is a good thing; who wants to be thought of as a 'stick in the mud'? And so it is; but just try going into the office tomorrow and saying 'Right, there are going to be some changes round here, now' and see what response you get. People, for the most part, make changes reluctantly. They do not like changing habits, they are fearful of making wrong decisions, and of the results of so doing. These are all good reasons for ensuring careful communication.

How feedback occurs   All the former would be easier if we always knew accurately what was going on, how much of the message was being taken in. But people often hide their reactions, and are protective about what they are thinking, at least in the short-term. This is true even to the point where feelings are actively disguised, a nod rather than a 'Yes' in fact indicating puzzlement rather than understanding or agreement.

What is generally happening here is that a message is being filtered as it is received. It is checked for validity, for relevance, to see if it relates to previous experience or clashes with any prejudices, and is then probably only accepted in diluted form. If the communication is good it will get through unscathed, or largely so; if not there are many hazards waiting to make it less effective.

As ex-President Nixon is attributed with saying: "I know that you understand what you think I said, but I am not sure you realize that what you heard is not what I meant."

All this means that the communicator, trainer in this case, must be careful to communicate in ways that will overcome all, or most, of these difficulties. Particularly, it is wise to:

- bear in mind the kind of audience you have, especially if in terms of beliefs or experience they are likely to see matters in a way that is different from yourself.
- make sure that the meaning of what you want to put across is clear; even the wrong or poor choice of one word can change what you want to say. I recently heard someone in a presentation describe his organization's 'fragmented range of services'. Whatever he meant (divisionalized for better communication with customers, perhaps), it was the wrong word, and the negative impact on those to whom he was speaking was all too clear. Yet it was just one word; greater confusion will place the message further off target. The danger of jargon, which is also relevant here, has already been mentioned.
- visual aids, which allow you to utilize two senses and add the variety of changing between one and the other, are clearly useful, and it is a rare training event that does not include any (this was gone into in some detail in Chapter 4).

Finally, also remember the principles by which learning takes place: effect, belonging and so on, which were explored in Chapter 2.

Enough of the difficulties, for the moment at least. What makes for a good presentation? There is one overriding factor: empathy, the ability to put yourself in the shoes of the participants. Most of what makes people say 'That's a good presenter' is down to this in one way or another. There is no academic measure – a good presentation is one that the audience like, and in a business context find useful; and in training, of course, the one from which they learn – preferably something of value – in an interesting way.

So we must think about how we see the audience (the group of trainees), and how they see us. As the latter is more straightforward, let us start with that.

HOW THE GROUP SEES YOU

Any trainer must direct the group, must be in charge, and must therefore look the part. There are some who hold that the trainer should always wear a suit, or the equivalent in terms of formality for a woman. There is some sense in this, and while there are no doubt exceptions, the relative positioning of the trainer with the group is usually important. Similarly, stand up as opposed to sitting (there may be some sessions that can be run while sitting, but not many. Not only does appearance differ, but most trainers will actually perform in a different and more stimulating manner when standing). If standing is the chosen option, stand up straight, do not move about too much, and present an appearance of purposefulness.

The trainer is the expert, is, or should be, in charge, and so appearance is a relevant factor.

HOW YOU SEE THE GROUP

How you view the group is not, of course, simply a visual point; what is necessary is an understanding of the group, and the individuals in it, and an appreciation of their point of view and their way of seeing things. Training demands decisions of people. Do I agree? Can I see the relevance of this? Shall I agree with this point? So it is necessary to understand the thinking process which takes place in the minds of those in the group in such circumstances.

This thinking follows a common sense sequence of seven stages. All are important to how a message is received, and a successful training session will incorporate them all. We now review these stages to illustrate how they affect what must be done.

1. *I am important*
We all regard ourselves as important, and what is more want others to recognize this importance. Unless the trainer is seen to respect members of the group, real learning will not take place. This process must occur directly in terms of normal courtesies, and in terms of the way to which the jobs, responsibilities and performance of the people are referred.

2. *Consider my needs*

Needs in terms of what people feel as individuals, and relative to the jobs they do (clearly, these are sometimes in conflict, as with something that will improve job performance but be difficult for the individual); both aspects are important. Attention will always be greater and more immediate if it is made absolutely clear how what is being presented relates to people's needs.

3. *Will your ideas help me?*

If what is being said is beginning to be seen as relevant, then an analysis takes place which asks if it is actually something to accept and implement, either literally or in some modified form. Does it, in fact, meet needs that exist?

4. *What are the facts?*

With much of what will be discussed at training sessions participants are not making snap judgements, though sometimes this will tend to happen, but are intent on weighing up the case to see whether they are convinced. They therefore want to know the facts, and they want them logically presented in a form that assists the weighing-up process. They ask themselves whether they have enough information, the right information, and whether they are clear about it – do they understand to a degree that will allow the lesson, whatever it is, to be implemented?

5. *What are the snags?*

There are always two sides to any argument. The phrase 'weighing up' used earlier was deliberately chosen; this is exactly what is happening. Members of the group will ask themselves both what are the reasons to accept this, and what are the points against? Often there are snags, but they do not necessarily rule out acceptance – on balance, they conclude, the case is good. Such snags perceived in this way need either to be anticipated and commented upon to redress the balance included in the presentation or, if reservations come up as questions, they need to be handled effectively with the same aim in mind. It is unrealistic to think that no objections will be raised.

6. *What shall I do?*

Here the process of implementation is also in play. In other words, having weighed up the case – assessed the balance – a participant not only needs to be able to say 'I accept that point', nor even 'I accept that point and will do it'; he needs to be able to say 'I accept that, I will do it and I can see how to do it'. The last point is important. How many good ideas are never implemented because people are not sure how to go about it? This is especially true of anything that has about it some genuine difficulty. To paraphrase G. K. Chesterton, who was writing about Christianity, it is not that some problems are tried and found wanting, it is that they are found difficult and therefore not tried.

7. *I accept*

The entire thinking process outlined above will only conclude positively if the process has been allowed, indeed encouraged, to proceed in this manner and sequence. What it is setting out is what people like to do, to some extent what their inherent reaction is to do. If it is going to happen then we have to work with it and use it to advantage.

Now remembering this, one of the dangers is at once apparent. This is the other person's point of view, and the trainer is as likely to focus on his own point of view as anyone else. You should ensure that you do not become introspective, concerned with your own views or situation; but instead to use and display enough empathy to come over as being constantly concerned about their view. This sounds obvious, but it is all too easy to find your perspective predominating, thus suffering a dilution of effectiveness. Even the most important message has to earn a hearing, and this is achieved primarily through concentrating on what is important to the group. Nervousness of the actual process of presenting training may compound this potential danger.

Next we turn to the structure of the presentation itself, and review how one goes through it. Probably the most famous of all maxims about any kind of communication is the old saying 'Tell'em, tell'em and tell'em'. This can be stated more clearly as meaning that you should tell people what you are going to tell them, tell them, and then tell them what it was you told them. This sound silly, perhaps, but compare it with something a little different, the way a good report is set out, for instance. There is an introduction, which says what it is that follows; there is the main body of the document, which goes progressively through the message; and the summary which, well, summarizes or says what has been covered. It is straightforward, but if it is ignored, messages may then go largely to waste.

So, practising to some degree what I preach, we now split the presentation into three sections, and see not only how to make each effective, but how to ensure that the three together make a satisfactory whole.

STRUCTURE OF THE PRESENTATION

Having said there are three stages – which we review under the more businesslike headings of the beginning, the middle and the end – we start with another, which is either confusing or an example of an intriguing opening. In any case, it has been referred to before – preparation.

Here I wish only to emphasize the point. Preparation is important; as Mark Twain once said, "It usually takes me three weeks to prepare a good impromptu speech." If he was half as good a speaker as he was a writer it makes a point. Here, as we review the stages, it is both the evidence for and the basis of the need for preparation. This has been referred to in an earlier chapter; however, it should be borne in mind as you read on. We shall now start, with appropriate logic, at the beginning, and see how each stage can be made easier.

Stage 1: The beginning

The beginning is clearly an important stage. People are uncertain, they are saying to themselves 'what will this be like?', 'will I find it interesting; helpful?'. They may also have their minds on other matters: what is going on back at the office, the job they left half finished, how will their assistant cope when they are away even for a day or two? This is particularly true when the peole in the group do not know you. They have no previous experience of what to expect, and this will condition their thinking (it is also possible that previous experience will make them wary!). With people you know well there is less of a problem, but the first moments of any session or programme are nevertheless always important.

It is not only important to the participants, it is important to the trainer; nothing settles the nerves – and even the most experienced speakers usually have a few qualms before they start – better than having a good start. Remember, the beginning is, necessarily, the introduction; the main objective is therefore to set the scene, state the topic (and rationale for it) clearly, and begin to discuss the 'meat' of the content. In addition, you have to obtain the group's attention – they will never learn if they are not concentrating and taking in what goes on – and create some sort of rapport both between you and the group, and around the group itself.

Let us take these aspects in turn.

● *Gaining attention*
  Primarily achieved by manner and the start you make. You have to look the part, your manner has to say 'this will be interesting', 'this person knows what they are talking about'. A little has been said about such factors as appearance, standing up, and so on. Suffice it to say here that if your start appears hesitant, the wrong impression will be given and, at worst, everything thereafter will be more difficult.

  More important is what you first say and how it is said. There are a number of types of opening, each presenting a range of opportunities for differing lead-ins. For example:

  – *a question:* rhetorical or otherwise, preferably something that people are likely to respond to positively:

    "Would you welcome a better way to . . . ?"
  – *a quotation:* which might be humorous or make a point, which might be a classic, or novel phrase; or it might be something internal:

    "At the last company meeting, the M.D. said . . ."
  – *a story:* again, something that makes a point, relates to the situation or people, or draws on a common memory:

    "We all remember the situation at the end of the last financial year when . . ."
  – *a factual statement:* perhaps striking, thought provoking, challenging or surprising:

    "Do you realize that this company receives 120 complaints every working day?" (the fact that this is also a question indicates that all these methods and more can be linked).
  – *a dramatic statement:* a story with a startling end, perhaps. Or a statement that surprises in some way:

One trainer, talking about direct mail advertising, started by asking the group to count, out loud and in unison, from 1–10. Between two and three he banged his fist down on the table saying 'Stop' loudly. "And that", he continued, "is how long your direct mail has to catch people's attention – 2½ seconds!"

– *an historical fact:* a reference back to an event which is a common experience of the group:

"In 1990, when company sales for what was then a new product were just . . ."

– *a curious opening:* simply a statement sufficiently odd for people to wait to find what on earth it is all about:

"Consider the aardvark, and how it shares a characteristic of some of our managers . . ." (in case you want a link, it is thick skinned).

– *a checklist:* perhaps a good start when placing the 'shopping list' in mind early on is important:

"There are 10 key stages to the process we want to discuss, first, . . ."

There must be more methods and combinations of methods that you can think of: whatever you pick, this element of the session needs careful, and perhaps more precise, preparation.

- *Creating rapport*
  At the same time, you need to ensure that an appropriate group feeling is started. In terms of what you say (participation also has a role here), you may want to set a pattern of 'we' rather than 'them and us'; in other words, say 'we need to consider . . .' and not 'you must . . .'. If this approach is followed then a more comfortable atmosphere is created; you may add – discreetly – a compliment or two ("As experienced people, you will . . ."); mention some common interest; mention some point to verify your competence in the area under discussion ("As an engineer myself . . ."), though without overt boasting; and above all, *be enthusiastic*.
  It is said that the one good aspects of life that is infectious is enthusiasm. Use it.

At the same time, the opening stages need to make it absolutely clear what the objectives are, what will be dealt with, and how it will benefit those present. It must also move us into the topic in a constructive way.

This opening stage is the first 'Tell'em' from 'Tell'em, tell'em and tell'em', and directs itself at the first two stages of the group's thinking process.

Stage 2: The middle

The middle is the core of the session. The objectives are clear:

- review of the content in detail
- ensure acceptance of the message
- maintain attention

and anticipate, prevent and, if necessary, handle objections.

One of the principles here is to take one point at a time; we shall do just that.

Putting over the content

The main trick here is to adopt a structured approach. Make sure you are dealing with points in a logical sequence; for instance, working through a process in a chronological order. And use what is referred to in communications literature as 'flagging', that is straight back to the three 'tell'ems'; you cannot say "There are three key points here; performance, method and cost; let's deal with them in turn. First, performance . . ." too much. Giving advance warning of what is coming, putting it in context, and relating it to a planned sequence, keeps the message organized and improves understanding.

This technique, and clarity give you the overall effect you want. People must obviously understand what you are talking about. There is no room for verbosity, for too much jargon, or for anything which clouds understanding. A pretty good measure of the trainer is when people afterwards feel that, perhaps for the first time, they really have come to understand clearly.

You cannot refer to manual excavation devices; in training a spade has to be called a spade. What is more, it has, as it were, to be an interesting spade if attention is to be maintained.

Maintaining attention

Some of the factors that are important here link with topics reviewed elsewhere. The principles are straightforward.

Keep stressing the relevance of what is being discussed to the participants. For instance, do not say that some matter will be a cost saving to the organization, stress personal benefits – will it make something easier, quicker or more satisfying to do, perhaps?

Make sure that the presentation remains visually interesting by using visual aids and demonstrations.

Use descriptions that incorporate stories, or anecdotes to make the message live. You cannot have too many anecdotes, and if your memory is less than perfect you will need a method of recording them and, just as important, accessing them.

Involve people, a topic investigated at some length in Chapter 6. As well as the techniques for creating participation reviewed there, it is necessary to have a participative attitude. The best trainers appear to digress, and take questions and involve people in a variety of unplanned ways; yet they finish on time, having dealt with the published content.

Finally, continue to generate attention through your own interest and enthusiasm.

Obtaining acceptance

People will only implement what they have come to believe is good sense. It is not enough to have put the message over, and have it understood: it has to be *believed*.

Here we must start by going back to understanding, nothing will be truly accepted unless this is achieved. Let us repeat here, to some extent better understanding is helped by:

- using clear, precise language – language which is familiar to those present, and which does not over-use jargon.
- making explanation clear, making no assumptions, using plenty of similes (you can hardly say 'this is like . . .' too often), and with sufficient detail to get the point across. One danger here is that in explaining points that you know well, you start to abbreviate, allowing your understanding to blind you as to how far back it is necessary to go with people for whom the message is new.
- demonstrations add considerably to the chances of understanding. These can be specific: product knowledge training can include an object lesson in assembling some object, for instance. In this case, the golden rule is (surprise, surprise) preparation. Credibility is immediately at risk if some demonstration does not work first time and in a straightforward manner. (This is a principle that is often not transferred; I regularly see people attempting to sell equipment, and yet failing to carry out an impressive – or even competent – demonstration.) Alternatively, a physical, visual demonstration may make a different point; like having someone describe how to tie a necktie to show the difficulty of voice only communication, as in telephone skills training.
- Visual aids are a powerful aid to understanding. As the old saying has it, 'a picture is worth a thousand words'; graphs make an excellent example of this, many people instantly understand a point from a clear graph which would usually elude them in a mass of figures. Visual aids have been commented on elsewhere.

It is not, however, just a question of understanding. As has been said, acceptance is also vital. Acceptance is helped by factors already mentioned (telling people how something will benefit them – or others they are concerned about, such as their staff), and the more specific this link can be made the better the effect will be on the view formed.

In addition, acceptance may only come once validity has been established, and this, in turn, may demand something other than your saying, in effect, "this is right". Validity can be improved by references, what other people say. A description that shows how well an idea or system has worked in another department and sets this out chapter and verse may be a powerful argument. Always with references this is dependent on the source of the reference being respected. If the other department are regarded in a negative way, then their adopting some process or product may be regarded by others as being a very good reason not to have anything to do with it. References work best when the results of what is being quoted are included so that the message says they did this and so and so has occurred since, with sufficient detail to make it interesting and credible.

Finally, it is worth making the point that you will not always know whether acceptance of a point has been achieved, at least not without checking. People cannot be expected to nod or speak out at every point, yet knowing that you have achieved acceptance may be important as you proceed. Questions to establish appropriate feedback are therefore a necessary part of this process. It is also advisable to keep an eye on the visible signs, watching, for instance, for puzzled looks.

Handling objections

The first aspect here is the anticipation, indeed the pre-emption, of objections. On occasions it is clear that some subject to be dealt with is likely, even guaranteed, to produce a negative reaction. If there is a clear answer then it can be built into the presentation, avoiding any waste of time. It may be as simple as a comment such as "Of course, this needs time, always a scarce resource, but once set up time will be saved; regularly", which then goes on to explain how this will happen.

Otherwise, if objections are voiced – and of course they will be – then a systematic procedure is necessary if they are to be dealt with smoothly.

First, give it a moment: too glib an answer may be mistrusted or make the questioner feel – or look – silly. So, pause . . . and for long enough to give yourself time to think (which you might just need), and give the impression of consideration. An acknowledgement reinforces this: "That's a good point", "We must certainly think about that", though be careful of letting such a comment become a reflex and seen as such. Then you can answer, with either a concentration on the individual's point and perspective, or with a general emphasis which is more useful to the group. Or both, in turn.

Very importantly, never, ever bluff. If you do not know the answer you must say so (no group expects you to be infallible), though you may well have to find out the answer later and report back. Alternatively, does anyone else know? Similarly, there is no harm in delaying a reply: "That's a good point, perhaps I can pick it up, in context, when we deal with . . .". More about questions, objections in any case being too strong a word for some, in the next chapter.

A final word here: beware of digression. It is good to answer any ancillary points that come up, but you can stray too far. Part of the training job is that of chairperson; everything planned has to be covered, and before the scheduled finishing time. If therefore, you have to draw a close to a line of enquiry, and you may well have to do so, make it clear that time is pressing. Do not ever let anyone feel it was a silly point to raise.

After all this, when we have been through the session, the time comes to close.

Stage 3: The end

Always end on a high note. The group expect it, if only subconsciously. It is an opportunity to build on past success during the session or, occasionally, to make amends for anything that has been less successful.

That apart, the end is a pulling together. However you finally end, with something as complex as a training session there is nearly always a need to summarize in an orderly fashion. This may well be linked to an action plan for the future, so that in wrapping up what has been said is reviewed – completing the 'Tell'ems' – and a commitment is sought as to what should happen next. This is important. Most people are under pressure for time and, whatever else, training takes time. They will be busier after even a day or two on a course than would be the case if they had not attended, so there is a real temptation to put everything on one side and get back to work – get back to normal. Yet this may be just where a little time needs to be put in to start to make some changes. Their having a real intention in mind as they leave the programme is not a guarantee that action will flow, but it is a start, and makes it that much more likely that something will happen, especially if there is follow up.

Like the beginning, there is then a need to find a way of handling, in this case, the final signing off. You can, for instance, finish with:

- *a question:* that leaves the final message hanging in the air, or makes it more likely that people will go on thinking about the issues a little longer:

  "I asked a question at the start of the session, now let us finish with another . . ."
- *a quotation:* that encapsulates an important, or the last, point:

  'Good communication is as stimulating as black coffee, and just as hard to sleep after" (Anne Morrow Lindberg),

  or, while not linked inextricably to the topic, a good closing lines is:

  "The more I practise, the more good luck I seem to have" (which is attributed to just about every famous golfer there is).
- *a story:* longer than the quotation, but with the same sort of intention. If it is meant to amuse, be sure it does; you have no further chance at the end to retrieve the situation. That said, I shall resist the temptation to give an example, though a story close does not only imply a humorous story.
- *an alternative:* this may be as simple as "will you do this or not?", or the more complicated options of a spelt out plan A, B or C.
- *immediate gain:* this is an injunction to act linked to an advantage of doing so now:

  "Put this new system in place and you will be saving time and money tomorrow" – more fiercely phrased, it is called a fear based end: "Unless you ensure this system is running you will not . . .". The positive route is usually better.

However you decide to wrap things up, the end should be a logical conclusion, rather than something separate added on the end.

All of this has much in common with the skills of any presentation. There is a difference, however. You want people not just to say that they enjoyed it, you want them to learn from it. The ways in which people learn are therefore important principles to keep in mind throughout. It needs patience as well as intellectual weight or 'clout'. It needs sensitivity to the feedback as well as the ability to come through it. As with many skills, the difficulty is less with the individual elements, most of which are straightforward and common sense, than with the orchestration of the whole process. The trainer must be able to present effectively, to remain flexible throughout, and work with the group rather than talking at them.

Remember the definition given early on: 'Training is helping people to learn': that means a particular kind of presentation is necessary, one that involves the group and the individuals in it. And this is the ultimate variable. People are inherently unpredictable, you never know quite what is going to happen. Add the management of this to the elements already reviewed, and we are really talking about working a group. This makes it sound like a manipulative process, which in a sense it is – though it should never appear so in any unpleasant way – participation must be constructive if it is to assist learning.

And it must be made to occur. There is nothing worse than the uneasy silence which can ensue if no comment, discussion or questions are forthcoming at the appropriate moment. How this aspect is added, seamlessly, to the whole is the subject of the next chapter.

Let us put ourselves into a participative mood – read on.

6 Running the session: Participative techniques

'What we have to learn to do, we learn by doing.'
Aristotle

The previous chapter looked at straightforward presentation factors; straightforward, at least, in the sense that we concentrated on the communication directed from the trainer to the participants. But training demands participation. Without it even the best presented session can become dull. More important, 'doing', rather than simply listening is more likely to produce both learning and retention, and therefore a subsequent change in behaviour.

This chapter describes a variety of participative techniques. It is not suggested that everything referred to should be used in every session; that would create an 'all singing, all dancing' effect, and total confusion. What is reviewed is more in the nature of a shopping list: you will recognize elements that are necessary in every session, others that are appropriate on an occasional basis. There is some, intentional, overlap with points made earlier in the book.

Participation may need introducing into sessions; if it does there is merit in introducing it early on. We shall start, therefore, logically, at the beginning.

FIRST IMPRESSIONS LAST

You only have one chance to make a good first impression. That may be a cliché, but it is important.

As has been said, a course leader is much more than simply a presenter. The job is normally more than imparting knowledge; you have to change behaviour, even attitudes. This may be a difficult job in any case; it will be doubly difficult if you do not have the participants' attention and interest. And obtaining this starts in the first few minutes.

It can even start before the session really begins. You know the awkward moments before start time: you are waiting for the last few attendees to arrive, and – particularly if you are busy with last minute preparations – their conversation may flag.

It is quite possible at this stage to start things off without actually starting the programme. For instance, even a simple *instruction* "Perhaps you would like to complete the name card in front of you before we start" will create some action. Alternatively, you can use some point to *prompt relevant conversation*; for instance: "Do introduce yourself to your immediate neighbours" (when they do not know each other, or not well), or "Do ask your neighbour how they see the programme briefing, what is the most important objective today?" (*Note:* if people do not know each other well, always use name cards so that everyone can address everyone else by name.)

Always start on time. You must lead by example in this respect, and running to time is important, not least to you in accordance with your planning. Your starting on time, completing what you intended for a session – in spite of any digressions – and finishing on time helps make what you are doing appear more professional.

So, on time, you begin. Immediately there are conflicting priorities. You need to deal with a variety of administrative points. Some, such as how you plan to handle questions, may be important to mention early on. You also need to come quickly to the 'meat' of the topic in a way that generates interest and rapport.

There is no 'best' sequence. Some trainers prefer to put the administration out of the way before starting on the training content. Some prefer to spend a moment generating interest, then dealing with the formalities almost as a digression, before coming back to the content.

The following section presents all the main elements of this stage in a logical order, but it is not the only possible order. You must decide for yourself with a particular session in mind.

A strong start is not only important in itself – it can set the scene for participation, perhaps by involving some people at once through questions, perhaps simply by creating an atmosphere that will make participation easier at a later stage. The methods described here provide many of these opportunities.

Some of the starting methods described in the last chapter are revisited in the box at the top of the next page.

How to start

The first statement may be:

● A question (actual or, more likely at this stage, rhetorical):	"Would you be interested in a way of ... ?"
● A quotation (attributable):	"Advertising may be described as the science of arresting human intelligence long enough to get money from it" Stephen Leacock
● A saying (not attributable):	'He is never lost for a few appropriated words'

(*Note:* carefully chosen quotations or sayings can be a safer way of introducing a slight element of humour than the 'funny story' – see page 34):

● A story:	"You may remember what happened when our last new product was launched . . ."
● A fact:	"Sales figures are at record levels"
● A historic reference:	"In 1979, when the company had achieved a million pound turnover for the first time . . ."

1. Welcome the participants to the sessions. Introduce yourself, and explain your role.
2. (If necessary) Ask participants to introduce themselves to the group – specifying exactly how, and how long, this should take.
3. Outline the course objectives, programme, timetable and methodology. This may usefully cover:

● *what* you will cover	"The coverage is . . ."
● perhaps also what you will *not* cover	"The intention is not to be comprehensive, but to concentrate on key areas . . ."
● *how* it will be done	"As you will have seen from the programme, whilst I shall lead the proceedings, there are exercises for you to do, a training film . . . and the session will end with some role play"
● *how* participation, particularly questions, will be handled	"I shall take questions and comments as we proceed, so do say if anything is not clear or . . ."
● a concise encapsulation of any *administrative* points	"Let me list quickly some of the admin points . . ."

(*Note:* This may include timings, dietary requirements, telephone and message procedures, where the toilets are located, fire precautions, duration of breaks and a word about strict timekeeping, etc.)

- *participants' notes* are often worth a special word, so that people do not spend time writing text that will be issued later.

"I shall let you have a clear résumé note at . . ."

4. Link what the course is about clearly and positively to the jobs of those present. Not just 'this is important', but 'this is important to you because . . .'.

   Most training is better received if it can be made motivational, and if it is positioned positively – making things better rather than correcting faults.

In addition, and the placing of this is also variable, you may need what is often called an 'ice-breaker'. This usually refers to an exercise which is there simply to start proceedings. It may puzzle, intrigue; it may make participants think, it may suprise them. Some only do this. For example:

- What letter comes next in the sequence O T T F F _____?
- Does F go above or below the line in the following?

(Answers are on page 80, just in case you need a moment to think!)

   The best ice-breakers, however, for any specific occasion, are on a topic, or have a moral, which links to the course content. They can be simple, like the following 'classic':

Ask participants to draw the following:

and join the dots using not more than four straight lines. Allow a couple of minutes.

The solution is:

Most see it as a box, and no solution is possible within the square. *Moral:* we must constantly seek solutions outside our immediate experience – the background emphasis of this course.

Alternatively, they can be longer and more complex. For instance, an excellent one involves making the teams complete two jigsaw puzzles (with only one of the pictures to guide them), and produces 20/30 minutes which demonstrates just about every aspect of leadership and teamwork you care to mention.

A final note; you should have the course well under way by this stage, but remember that your approach, confidence, style and so on are saying a great deal to people in these first minutes. They go through the first 10 minutes or half an hour saying to themselves "what can this person teach me?", "can I see myself usefully spending an hour, or a day or two, in their company?"

If you are dealing with a matter of which you have personal experience, it may be desirable to drop into the introductions some point that demonstrates your own competence, some anecdote perhaps – it need not suggest you are the best in the world at whatever it is, but it should suggest that you know your subject well. There is a saying, 'that you don't need to be able to lay eggs to be a chicken farmer', but it does help to know the backside from the beak.

We turn now to the formal, presentational, inputs.

INVOLVING PEOPLE

There is a story of someone coming home after a course. Their spouse asks "What was it like?", and they reply "It was good. I spoke". People like to be involved. They can often learn as much from each other, from the thinking generated by questions, discussion, exercises and so on as from the formal inputs. Consider questions first.

Taking questions

The first decision is when to take questions. This can be seen as a compromise because:

- questions allowed at any time can disrupt the planned balance of a presentation, unless you exercise control;
- delaying questions to the very end can frustrate the group, and give you a false sense of security that the earlier points have been accepted;
- discouraging questions, or leaving no time for them, is poor training.

You may therefore plan to take questions after each main point. Whatever you do, tell the group the rules; allow time in the presentation for the chosen methodology to work.

As you handle questions *from* the group, you may find it useful to use the following techniques:

- acknowledge the question and questioner;
- ensure, as necessary, that the question is heard and understood by the rest of the group;
- if in doubt as to what is meant, probe to clarify and restate it back if necessary;

- give short informative answers whenever possible. Link to other parts of your message, as appropriate.

If you opt, which you may want to, for questions at any time, remember it is perfectly acceptable to:

- hold them for a moment until you finish making a point;
- delay them; saying you will come back to it, in context in, say, the next session. (Then you must remember. Make a note of both the point and who made it.);
- refuse them. Some may be irrelevant or likely to lead to too much of a digression, but be *careful* not to do this too often, to respect the questioner's feelings, and to explain why you are doing so;
- and if you don't know the answer, you *must* say so. You can offer to find out, you can see if anyone else in the group knows, you can make a note of it for later, but if you attempt, unsuccessfully, to answer you lose credibility. No-one, in fact, expects you to be omniscient, so do not worry about it: if you are well prepared it will not happen often in any case.

Asking questions

The questions you ask can check understanding, or prompt discussion, and make the group think round a point, building their understanding. They will retain information better if there is an element of finding out involved in its acquisition rather than only 'being told'.

Questions must be put *precisely*. There is an(other) apocryphal story of the question which asks people 'Are you in favour of smoking whilst praying?', this does not sound very good, and most people will say 'No'. But ask 'Are you in favour of praying whilst smoking?', however, and most will say 'Yes' (is there a time when one should not pray?). Yet both phrases concern the simultaneous carrying out of the two actions. The moral is to be careful to ask the question in the right way, or you may not obtain the answer you want.

Many questions are best phrased as *open questions*. These cannot be answered yes or no, and so are more likely to prompt discussion. They typically start what, why, where, who, how or, in training, can be neatly led into by asking people to:

describe	explain	discuss . . . . .
justify	clarify	illustrate . . . . .
outline	verify	define . . . . .
review	compare	critique . . . . .

Answers (from page 78)

- O T T F F S – *one, two, three, four, five, six.*
- F goes above the line, as do all those letters made up of straight lines: ones with curves are below the line.

There are several ways of directing questions; they can be:

- *Overhead questions*, put to the group generally, and useful for opening up a subject (if there is no response, then you can move on to the next method):

  "Right, what do you think the key issue here is? Anyone?"
- *Overhead and then directed at an individual*, useful to make the whole group think before looking for an answer from one person:

  "Right, what to you think the key issues here are? Anyone? . . . John, what do you think?"
- *Direct to individual*, useful for obtaining individual responses, testing for understanding:

  "John, what do you think . . . ?"
- *Non-response/rhetorical*, useful where you want to make a point to one or more persons in the group without concentrating on anyone in particular, or for raising a question you would expect to be in the group's mind and then answering it yourself:

  "What's the key issue? Well, perhaps it's . . ."

All these methods represent very controlled discussion, i.e. leader . . . team member . . . leader . . . another team member (or more), but . . . back to the leader. Two other types help to open up a discussion:

- *Re-directed questions*, useful to make others in the group answer any individual's answer:

  "That's a good point John. What do you think the answer is, Mary?"
- *Developmental questioning*, where you take the answer to a previous question and move it around the audience, building on it:

  "Having established that, how about . . . ?"

Whichever of the above is being used, certain principles should be borne in mind. For questioning to be effective, the following general method may be a useful guide to the kind of sequence that can be employed:

- *State the question clearly and concisely.* Questions should relate directly to the subject being discussed. Whenever possible they should require people to think, to draw on their past experiences, and relate them to the present circumstances.
- *Ask the question first to the group rather than to an individual.* If the question is directed to a single individual, others are off the hook and do not have to think about the answer. Direct, individual questions are more useful to break a general silence in the group, or to involve someone who is not actively participating in the discussion.
- *After asking the question, pause.* Allow a few moments for the group to consider what the answer should be. Then . . .

- *Ask a specific individual to answer.* The four-step process starts the entire group thinking because they never know who will be called on. Thus everyone has to consider each question you ask, and be ready to participate. Even those who are not called on are still involved.

To be sure of using an effective questioning technique, there are some points which should be avoided, such as:

- *Asking yes or no questions.* Participants can attempt to guess the answer (and may be right). These questions should not be used if you want participants to use their reasoning power and actively participate in the training.
- *Asking tricky questions.* Remember, your purpose is to train people, not to antagonize them or make them look bad. Difficult questions, yes. Tricky, no. Keep personalities and sarcasm out of your questions.
- *Asking unanswerable questions.* You want to provide knowledge, not confusion. Be sure that the knowledge and experience of your group are such that at least some participants can answer the questions you're asking. Never attempt to highlight ignorance by asking questions which the group can't handle.

  And this is particularly true when you're trying to draw out a silent trainee and involve them. Be sure they can answer before you ask them the questions.
- *Asking personal questions.* Personal questions are usually rather sensitive, even in one-to-one sessions. They are often inappropriate in a group session.
- *Asking leading questions.* By leading questions, we mean ones in which the trainer indicates the preferred answer in advance: "Mary, don't you agree that this new form will help solve the problem?" Such questions require little effort on the part of the participant, and little learning takes place. In addition, even if Mary didn't agree, she would probably be uncomfortable saying so. After all, that does not seem to be the answer you want.
- *Repeating questions.* Don't make a practice of repeating the question for an inattentive person. Doing so simply encourages further inattention and wastes valuable time. Instead, ask someone else to respond. People will quickly learn that they have to listen.
- *Allowing group answers.* Unless written down (and then referred to around the group), questions that allow several members of the group to answer are not useful. First, everyone cannot talk at once. Second, with group answers a very few participants may well tend to dominate the session. And third, group answers allow the silent person to hide and not participate as they should.

Note: the one unbreakable rule all training sessions should have, clearly understood and adhered to, is ONLY ONE PERSON MAY TALK AT ONCE (and the leader must be the acknowledged referee and decide who has the floor at any particular moment).

Above all, let your questioning be natural. Ask because you want to know – because you want this information to be shared with the group. Never think of yourself as a quiz master with certain questions that must be asked whether or not they're timely. Let your manner convey your interest in the response you're going to get, and be sure that your interest is genuine. Forced, artificial enthusiasm will never fool a group.

No matter how effective your questioning technique may become, never consider yourself so clever that you can manipulate the participants. Manipulation is not its purpose. Instead, questioning should be used to promote and build genuine participation, not in bending the group to your will.

Finally, for questioning to be an effective instructional technique you must create the proper atmosphere in which it can flourish. For example, participants should never fear to give an incorrect answer. If wrong answers are discouraged, participants will respond more cautiously. People should never have the feeling that they are asking stupid questions. It cannot be over-emphasized that they should be encouraged to ask questions, at any time, about anything they do not understand.

Using exercises

Questions can prompt discussion, which is valuable in two ways:

- people like, and learn from, participation as a process;
- the discussion may well be creative, casting new light on some aspect of the subject;

but, people will learn still more from actually working at a task.

Exercises can be as short as a few minutes or as long as many hours. For the purposes of the present discussion, which relates primarily to short training sessions of perhaps three hours to three days, exercises can be conducted in several ways:

- *individually:* there is a place for participants individually working through an exercise: one benefit is that of letting people work at their own pace, and on their own situations or problems. Protracted individual exercises in a group situation *seem* to be inappropriate, and are therefore best kept short.
- *in pairs:* working in pairs gives some of the advantages of individual exercises, yet involves active participation. It is affected by room layout, and works best when people are seated so that they can simply turn to their neighbours and go straight into an exercise without moving. (Additionally, an individual exercise can then be commented on, or developed in pairs).
- *in syndicates:* working in syndicates takes somewhat longer, and may involve some moving about, but it is useful. There should not be too many in a group, 5–8 perhaps, and you can make it work best by suggesting that:
  - a chairperson is promptly elected (or nominated) to control discussion and keep an eye on the time;
  - a secretary is chosen to keep notes of points agreed;
  - a presenter is chosen to report back to the main group.

If each exercise has a different chairperson or presenter, everyone is given an active role as syndicate sessions progress, and tasks are spread round the group.

The ultimate form of exercise, particularly for training in interactive skills (e.g. selling, communication, interviewing, counselling, etc.) is role playing. This needs careful setting up, and is worth considering in more detail before we move on.

Role playing

Role playing is a very powerful technique, though not necessarily the easiest activity to organize. If role playing is to be valuable it needs to be used carefully. It does provide practice in a 'safe' environment: if you are practising selling, interviewing or presentational techniques, for instance, it avoids upsetting real customers, audiences or applicants.

At its simplest, role playing is just the informal enactment of a real life situation. Say you are training in interviewing skills, you pose a question that leads into conversation: "Imagine the applicant says . . ." and you quote: "What would you reply?" This question, directed at one of the participants with an injunction to reply *verbatim*, creates a moment of conversation, one which can either be between you and the participant, or between two participants. These conversations carry along between the two parties for a moment or two, or for a few minutes, and then the session returns to normal. This is role playing; people are made to think about the topic, not in academic terms, but very much in its day-to-day application. Yet there is no formality, none of the equipment, recording and playback more normally associated with role playing.

At the other end of the scale there is considerable formality, with all the panoply of equipment and recording which can be daunting. I have been involved in role playing which returns in four main sessions during the day to the same developing scenario, which even uses people from outside the course and the organization (this, for example, in training in recruitment interviewing skills, where real interviews with actual candidates have been filmed – with the permission of the candidates – to assist in developing key skills); so elaborate forms are certainly possible, and can work well.

To return to the more routine, and start with the dangers, role playing can fail and, if it does, the cause probably lies among the following:

- over-awareness of the camera;
- over-acting to the camera;
- a belief that role playing means acting;
- the difficulty of 'performing' in front of one's peers;
- poor role play briefs;
- weak management of the role play;
- incomplete or unconstructive feedback after the role play;
- those not role playing being given nothing to do.

More positively, all role plays should be organized to achieve one or more of the following objectives:

- reproduce real life as closely as possible;
- provide an opportunity to practise difficult situations;
- provide an opportunity to practise new skills;
- develop confidence;
- enhance learning by building on success;
- experiment with new approaches;
- change negative habits/reinforce positive habits;

- fix knowledge and an attitude of professionalism;
- promote analytical skill through self-appraisal and observing others.

The following details four different forms of role playing which, although these can be adapted, amended and used in a variety of different ways, make useful examples, and show how to make role playing work well and generate constructive feedback. Though I have described them in terms of video use, there is no reason why they should not be effective without this facility.

The 'classic' role play This is where two participants act out a situation to reinforce an interactive skill. Assuming a clear objective, and the use of standard video equipment (i.e. camera/tripod, microphone, video recorder and TV monitor), the physical arrangements must be able to comfortably facilitate what needs to take place. The following examples show how this can be achieved. Though, of course, no one sequence of events should be followed slavishly, the following illustrates a typical approach:

- Issue the role play briefs to the two participants, and allow them time to plan their approaches. If either is playing themselves this should be made clear. It is certainly less confusing if participants use their own names, whatever their roles.
- State the objective, and summarize the briefs for the observers.
- Issue any observation and feedback forms to the observers. (A specific, sales training, example appears in Figure 6.1). Emphasize that theirs is an active role in the learning process.
- Introduce the camera operator (if one is used). Brief him on what he should capture on film, i.e. one participant's role, the others' reactions, or both.
- Indicate when you want the role play to end, i.e. after a certain time, or when a particular point in the content has been reached.
- Invite questions, ensuring that everyone knows what to do.
- Emphasize that a role play is a *group* learning exercise, not an opportunity to test one individual.
- Invite the two role players to take their places. (Layout needs some thought, examples appear in Figure 6.2).
- Take your seat near the video deck, and be prepared to note down the tape numbers of where key points occur during the exchanges (see the form in Figure 6.3).
- When the role play has finished:
  - thank the two participants and invite them to rejoin the group;
  - ask the observers to complete their feedback notes;
  - ask the two participants to write down their own impressions of their role play;
  - allow the lead player to comment first, drawing in the other as appropriate;
  - ask the observers to offer their initial impressions;
  - offer your own initial impressions;
  - play back the opening moments of the role play, using this as your cue to lead a discussion on particular details;

Figure 6.1   Observation and feedback form

	A+	A	B+	B
Participants: Salesman _____ Customer _____				
Role play objective: _____				
How well did the salesman listen to the customer?	[ ]	[ ]	[ ]	[ ]
How well did the salesman's replies satisfy the customer?	[ ]	[ ]	[ ]	[ ]
How clear and understandable were the salesman's questions?	[ ]	[ ]	[ ]	[ ]
How well did the salesman control the interview?	[ ]	[ ]	[ ]	[ ]
What was the salesman's level of product knowledge?	[ ]	[ ]	[ ]	[ ]
What was the salesman's level of competitor product knowledge?	[ ]	[ ]	[ ]	[ ]
How well did the salesman use his sales aids?	[ ]	[ ]	[ ]	[ ]
How well did the salesman spot and use opportunities to conclude the interview positively?	[ ]	[ ]	[ ]	[ ]

General impressions: _____

_____

Recommendations: _____

_____

- ensure that the observers' feedback is constructive, and the participants are allowed to respond;
- use the video to highlight key points;
- at an appropriate point, draw the discussions to a close. Ask for final comments from the observers; invite final comments from the participants and then summarize.

  Your summary should be divided into distinct elements: thank and praise the participants; thank the observers; summarize the key learning points which first, directly affect the individual(s), and second, may apply to the group.
- Re-wind the tape and prepare for the next role play.

Figure 6.2 Layout organization using only the training room

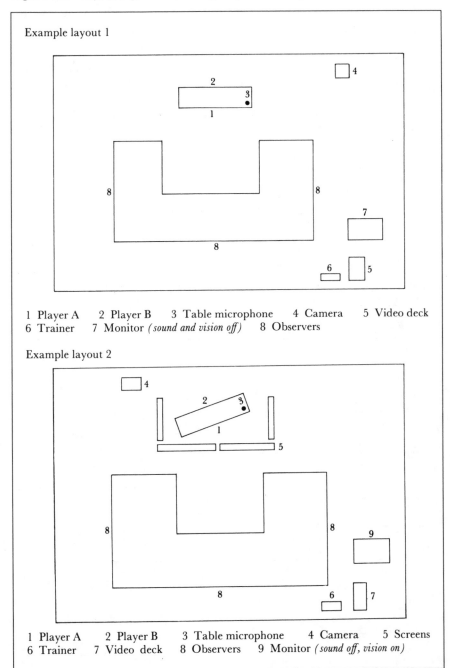

Example layout 1

1 Player A   2 Player B   3 Table microphone   4 Camera   5 Video deck
6 Trainer   7 Monitor *(sound and vision off)*   8 Observers

Example layout 2

1 Player A   2 Player B   3 Table microphone   4 Camera   5 Screens
6 Trainer   7 Video deck   8 Observers   9 Monitor *(sound off, vision on)*

Figure 6.3   Video tape number record form

Tape nos.		Actions/words	
From	To	Person A	Person B

The 'carousel' role play   This role play involves the situation being started by two participants and, at an appropriate point, being handed over to two others, who continue to act out the same scenario. It is thus a good way of involving more people in the group, more quickly.

Again, a typical but not definitive sequence of events illustrates what is involved:

- Divide the complete process into suitable parts (e.g. a sales interview might be divided into the opening, establishing needs, presenting the product/service, handling objections, and gaining a commitment; an interview, more simply, might be organized into a beginning, a middle and the conclusion.) Ensure that the group understands the basis for the split.
- Divide the group into pairs, and nominate who in each pair will play which role. However, do *not* indicate the phase which each pair will role play, not least so that everyone will concentrate throughout the proceedings.
- Distribute the Carousel Role Play Instructions (see example in Figure 6.4).
- Distribute any necessary Role Play Briefs. (*Note:* all members of the group should be given the same two briefs, one for each of the roles.)
- Invite or nominate two participants to play the first interview phase.
- Begin the role play.
- At an appropriate point, stop the role play and either:
    - (i)   invite a second pair to continue from that point, or
    - (ii) play back and take feedback comments, then invite a second pair to continue.
- When the complete scenario has been role played, lead a feedback discussion in the same way as for the 'classic' role play.

The 'silent' role play   Silent because the scenario is enacted in writing. This is clearly unsuited to anything lengthy, but is very valuable when there is great precision necessary (e.g. the brief moments when a prospecting sales person introduces his company on the telephone; the summary in a discipline interview where the wording must be exactly right).

Again, a typical sequence of events illustrates the process:

- Divide the group into pairs, and brief them about their respective roles. Check that all is clear.
- Then a conversation is acted out and written down – word for word. This is done on the same sheet of paper – passed between the two – so that the developing conversation remains visible in its entirety.
- Once the exchanges are complete the whole conversation can be read out and discussed. (*Note:* This also works well with the trainer playing one role and inter-relating with individual members of the group; and also with syndicates discussing, and recording, a measured response.)
- There should be *no* talking between parties during the role play.
- The real learning will take place during and after the role play; it teaches the importance of thinking about, clearly expressing and logically structuring what you want to say. Seeing the actual words in black and white can be an object lesson in learning how to focus and clarify spoken presentations.

Figure 6.4 Carousel role playing instructions

Objectives

To reinforce skill at _____
To actively involve everyone

1. One of our typical inverviews has been broken down into its key phases:
   (i) _____   (iii) _____
   (ii) _____   (iv) _____
2. Each pair will role play one of these phases.
3. You all have a copy of the same two briefs, one for each role.
4. The first pair will role play the first interview phase. At an appropriate point their role play will be stopped and a second pair will be invited to *continue the interview without losing its direction and building upon what has already been established.* This pair will role play the second interview phase.
5. Again, at an appropriate point this role play will be stopped and a third pair will be invited to *continue the same interview, also without losing direction and building upon the facts and agreements already established.* Their task is to role play the third interview phase.
6. *You must remain alert,* listening and taking notes so that, whenever it is your turn to take over you are able to *maintain the interview momentum.*
7. Throughout the interview you may introduce new information. However, if you do, this *must:*

   - not be designed to 'catch out' the other 'player'
   - not directly contradict whatever has already been established and agreed
   - sensibly reflect real life situations

8. The role plays will continue until a clear conclusion has been reached.
9. The trainer may temporarily halt the role play between pairs either to play back the video recording or to summarize key agreements between the two parties.

The 'triad' role play   As the name suggests, this involves three people participating in three roles during the role play session (e.g. a sales person and sales manager visiting a customer; an appraisal meeting at which a subordinate, a manager and an observer – perhaps a personnel person – is present).

This can either work very like the 'classic' role play, or the third person can be an observer (but staying 'in character'); thus, the role play observer's task is to observe, then comment upon the two role play participants. (Essentially, he plays the trainer.)

The remainder of the group have a dual task: to comment on the role play participants; and to watch and comment on how the observer conducts his feedback.

In the next role play, the observer moves into participant 'A's' seat, and A moves to the other side of the table and becomes 'B'. 'B' rejoins the group, and a new player takes over as observer (i.e. an element of carousel).

The trainer's role is to orchestrate the action and learning, not forgetting that the emphases in this type of role playing are: the participants and the skills displayed, and the observer and his analysis and appraisal skills.

From the least formal format, mentioned earlier, to the more complex, role playing is an important tool of training. It should not, however, be underestimated in terms of the care and preparation it necessitates. If it moves off track, if it goes badly, then people are made to look inadequate which, understandably, they do not like. Providing participants are clear as to the brief, and understand the purpose of the exercise, and providing that the trainer sets up the situation carefully and makes it a risk free experience, it can add to a training session to a meaningful extent. Its greatest contribution is not in providing a test of individuals, but in creating discussion of examples and situations which the whole group can use, and from which approaches for the future can be constructed.

Finally in this section, there should be a recognition that not all the people in any group are the same. Everyone is an individual, everyone responds to the group situation differently; but you have to work with them all.

Different people

As someone once observed, training would be easy if it were not for the participants. Whilst all are understandably different, some present problems. These problems must be tackled firmly, if only because by their attitude or characteristics people may not only fail to learn as much themselves as you would wish; they may also disrupt things for other members of the group.

The following snapshots suggest cures designed to direct problem participants – tactfully – back to the discussion at hand:

- The '*show-off*'
  Avoid embarrassing or shutting them off; you may need them later.
  Solution: toss him a difficult question. Or say, *"That's an interesting point. Let's see what the group thinks of it."*
- The '*quick reactor*'
  Can also be valuable later, but can keep others out of the discussion.
  Solution: thank him; suggest we put others to work.
- The '*heckler*'
  This one argues about every point being made.
  Solution: Remain calm. Agree, affirm any good points, but toss bad points to the group for discussion. They will be quickly rejected. Privately try to find out what's bothering him, try to elicit his cooperation.
- The '*rambler*'
  Who talks about everything except the subject under discussion.
  Solution: At a pause in his monologue, thank him, return to and restate relevant points of discussion, and go on.
- The '*mutual enemies*'
  When there is a clash of personalities.
  Solution: Emphasize points of agreement, minimize differences. Or frankly ask that personalities be left out. Draw attention back to the point being made.

- *The 'pig-headed'*
  He absolutely refuses, perhaps through prejudice, to accept points being discussed.
  Solution: Throw his points to the group, have them straighten him out. Tell him time is short, that you'll be glad to discuss it with him later.
- *The 'digresser'*
  Who takes the discussion too far off track.
  Solution: Take the blame yourself. Say, *"Something I said must have led you off the subject; this is what we should be discussing . . ."*
- *The 'professional gripe'*
  Who makes frankly political points.
  Solution: Politely point out that we cannot change policy here; the objective is to operate as best we can under the present system. Or better still, have a member of the group answer him.
- *The 'whisperers'*
  Who hold private conversations, which while they could be related to the subject, are distracting.
  Solution: Dot not embarrass them. Direct some point to one of them by name, ask an easy question. Or repeat the last point and ask for comments.
- *The 'inarticulate'*
  Who has the ideas, but can't put them across.
  Solution: Say, *"Let me repeat that . . . (then put it in better language)."*
- *The 'mistaken'*
  Who is clearly wrong.
  Solution: Say, *"That's one way of looking at it, but how can we reconcile that with . . . (state the correct point)?"*
- *The 'silent'*
  Who could be shy, bored, indifferent, insecure, or he just might learn best by listening.
  Solution: Depends on what is causing the silence. If bored or indifferent, try asking a provocative question, one you think he might be interested in. If shy, complement him when he *does* say something, and then ask him direct questions from time to time to draw him in.

And even if these *problem* situations do not occur, we should remember to:

- *Keep discussion on track*
If the group has got off the track, say, *"We've had some very interesting thoughts here, but let's see if we can't get an answer to our original question."*
  Or ask follow-up questions which call for an answer leading back to the topic.
- *Prevent discussion trailing into silence*
  If just *one person* is off the track, ask him how his point contributes to the topic under discussion. If it doesn't, he'll probably drop it.
  Stimulate by asking follow-up questions like:

  "Why"
  "What is your experience on that, John?"
  "Will you give us an example?"

"Why will it work?"
"Is there anything else we can do to make it work?"

- *Keep an eye on individuals*
  Whenever you can, remember or note who says what, when they make a good point, or have to be put down. For instance, if discussion has to be cut on one topic, simply because of time, cutting off someone anxious to make a comment, make sure they are an early participant in the next discussion to take place.

And that, as you should probably rarely say on a training session, is all there is to it. It is not everything, of course, but we have reviewed some of the key issues; besides, it is a broad topic. If you run these kinds of session and are conscious of how you go about it, and how it is received, you will spend a lifetime fine-tuning what you do. Not only does what you do improve with practice, but there is no 'right' way, you have to do it in your own style and adapt, at least to some degree, meeting by meeting, group by group.

Whatever you do, creating and handling participation will always be a vital element, indeed a key influence on how the whole event goes. You cannot really have too much participation; but the content must be allowed to shine through, and participation must be there for a reason. It must support the proceedings rather than becoming an end in itself. There is a danger that the reflex can become one of 'if in doubt, get them to do something', reminiscent of the old story about how many trainers it takes to change a light bulb. Answer; none, they simply assemble two syndicates, one to get the old bulb out, the other to put the new one in.

However, if you are well prepared, start the session off well, work at putting your message over clearly, and *involve people*, using the group to help the group and yourself, then you will find you are genuinely helping people to learn.

Just one more thing . . .

FINALLY

Always have the last word. Right at the end when you close the session the sequence is not – summary, any final questions, close; it is – indication of the end, any last questions, summary and close. It is the same principle which says you should never finish a meeting with the ubiquitous 'Any Other Business', but send people away on a high note. Within the summary and close a word of thanks for the participants' input may well be appropriate.

Rather like the opening remarks, closing remarks need to be well prepared. A summary should be just that. A closing remark may be:

- A question   "We started with a question, let's end with another . . ."
- A quotation or saying "A picture's worth a thousand words, they say – one final slide to summarize . . ."

- A story   "Let me tell you a brief story which illus-
                                   trates . . ."
- A summary   "There are three key points to bear in mind as we
                                   close. First, . . ."
- An alternative   "Right, so you can either opt for . . . or . . ."
- A call for action   ". . . and I suggest we start right now.."

Some of these can be used in combination, and you may well be able to think of others.

And remember that *ending on time*, or even with a little time in hand, is even more important than starting on time.

So, bearing everything covered so far in mind, your next training session is going to be the best you have ever done. No? Well, you could read the material in this book again (bearing in mind repetition and retention), prepare carefully, and *then* the next session you run will be the best ever. And, more important, it will really 'help people to learn'.

But even when all has apparently gone well there is another stage. In the next and final chapter we consider what happens *after* the session.

7   Following up

'Whatever is worth doing at all is worth doing well'
Earl of Chesterfield

What do you do when the session is over? Heave a sigh of relief (and start preparing tomorrow's session)? Pour yourself a large gin and tonic or a cold beer? Sit down? Perhaps all three sound like a good idea; training is supposed to burn up a lot of calories (though I have no scientific proof or personal evidence of that). The main theme of this book has been the session itself, planning, conceiving and conducting it, but it would be a nonsense to pretend that the process stops once the clock hits five o'clock.

Two points are of particular importance once the session is over: first, some kind of evaluation; and second, the link to any follow-up training or other work. We shall review these one at a time.

EVALUATION

Evaluation is important for a number of reasons:

- your own satisfaction (not least);
- the motivation of participants, who see the course or session as a more serious event if it is being monitored;
- to provide feedback that will help the creation of further similar training or improve repeats of the same session for other groups;
- to test that learning has taken place;
- to communicate with others in the organization, e.g. the managers of those attending the session;
- to gather sensible suggestions;
- and possibly to aid individual assessment (though this must be done carefully; people will resent their perhaps informal or experimental participation being used for assessment purposes and, in any case, it is difficult to concentrate on running a session and on every detail of individual performance).

There are four main types of evaluation; reaction evaluation; learning evaluation; performance evaluation; and impact evaluation.

Reaction evaluation

This type of evaluation measures the reaction of the participants to the session and the elements of it that are investigated. To an extent, this is the archetypal 'course assessment form', which asks whether people were satisfied with the course and why. It poses questions such as:

- What did you like most about the course?
- What did you dislike most?
- Did it achieve its objectives?
- How could it be improved?

These are general questions, but a good deal of useful information can be gleaned this way. Figures 7.1 – 7.5 show the variety of ways in which information can be obtained quite simply.

A word about ratings scales, which are a regular feature of such forms, should be noted. Always use an *even* number of ratings. The reason may be obvious, but can be overlooked. An even number has no mid-point, or, in other words, no average column. Give people an average column and many will mark everything blandly down the middle, either to avoid being harsh, or sometimes to avoid overt flattery. Either way, stick to an even number; four serves most purposes well. (It is true that the NTI forms illustrated in Figure 7.1 and 7.2 contain five – but perhaps that proves that, as George Bernard Shaw put it, the only golden rule is that there is no golden rule.)

Learning evaluation

This form of evaluation actually tests changes in the participants' knowledge, skills or attitudes, comparing this prior to and after the course in some cases, or just giving a test after the session. Knowledge, or the measurement of it, is clearly the most susceptible to this. A test of knowledge is not difficult to work out and must, of course, be particular to the individual session run.

Imagine a test based on this chapter. A learning evaluation would ask such questions as:

- list seven reasons why evaluation of a training session is important, or
- how many reasons for evaluating a training session can you think of?

or more simply, listing factors to tick. In fact, there are a variety of different ways of asking questions, from simple questions as above, to the completion of sentences, marking statements True or False, or using multiple choice. Even attitudes can be measured a certain amount, for instance by using a scale such as:

Strongly agree – Agree – Disagree – Strongly disagree

though as has been said, this is more difficult to do with certainty.

Figure 7.1 National Training Index: external course appraisal form

NATIONAL TRAINING INDEX

External course appraisal form

Your Company/Organisation is a subscribing member of the National Training Index. So that it can get the full benefit from its membership <u>IT IS VITAL</u> that you complete this form as fully as possible, and return it to your training officer.

A   The course

Title

Run by (name of organisation running the course)

Brief description of syllabus

No. of people present on the course

Principal speaker(s)

Dates

Fees (Please state whether this included cost of accommodation)

Where was the course held

B   The course member

Name

Age

Job title

Department

Company

Location

C   Summary report (You may find it helpful to complete section D overleaf before giving your summary report)

Finally it would be most useful if you would summarise your opinion of the course by grading it on a 1-5 scale, ticking in the box below as appropriate.

5 = Very Good
4 = Good — minor points of detail could be improved
3 = Average
2 = Only satisfactory, room for considerable improvement
1 = Weak

	5	4	3	2	1
General achievement of objectives:					
Effectiveness of the speakers Name					
Name					
Name					
Name					
Name					
Supporting paper-work					
Administration (timekeeping, accommodation, etc.)					

Please turn over

Figure 7.1   National Training Index: external course appraisal form – concluded

D   Written appraisal

Would you please expand on the strong and weak points of the course? It will be most helpful if you can consider these comments on the basis of answers to the following questions. We are particularly interested in your answer to Question 2. The fuller the comments you feel able to make, the more comprehensive will be the reports that can be compiled.

1 (a) What were the stated objectives of the course?
   (b) To what extent were these achieved?
   (c) Was the course content what you were expecting? If not, how did it differ from your expectations?

2 (a) What were the most useful parts of the course for you?
   (b) How will you apply them in your present post?

3 (a) What, if any sessions would you omit, and why?
   (b) What, if anything, would you like added to the course syllabus?

4 (a) What did you think of the standard of instruction?
   (b) Were any of the speakers particularly good, or weak?

5 For which type of delegate (age, job-title, experience) was the course most suited?

6 Was the course cost effective, in terms of the benefit you derived from attending, measured against what it cost your employers, both in fees and having you away from work?

7 How adequate were the administrative arrangements (accommodation, time-keeping, supporting paper-work, visual aids, etc.)

I authorise you to make use of this report to such extent as you may think fit for the purpose of compiling records and other publications of the National Training Index, and to enter as my agent into such agreements with subscribers as you may consider necessary in order to protect me from any legal liability in respect of any inaccuracy or other defect in this report, whether arising through negligence or otherwise.

Signature   **Date**

Figure 7.2 National Training Index: in-company training appraisal form

NATIONAL TRAINING INDEX
In-Company training appraisal form

This form is for completion by the Training Manager/Officer, NOT by individual delegates.

A   The course

Title or Subject

Run by (name of training organisation concerned)

Brief description of syllabus

No. of delegates attending

Names of the lecturers

Fee charged

Where was the course held (please state whether on your company's premises, or at a different location)

Dates and Duration of Course

B   Summary report

It would be most useful if you will summarise your opinion of the course by grading it on a 1-5 scale, ticking in the appropriate box below.

5 = Very good
4 = Good — minor points of detail could be improved
3 = Average
2 = Satisfactory, room for improvement
1 = Weak

	5	4	3	2	1
General achievement of objectives:					
Effectiveness of the lecturers: Name					
Name					
Name					
Preliminary survey work and consultation with company training staff					
Adherence to agreed course syllabus					
Supporting paperwork					
Follow-up proposals					

Please turn over

Figure 7.2   National Training Index: in-company training appraisal form – concluded

---

C   Written appraisal

Your answers to the following questions will enable the Index to compile informative in-company training reports. The more detailed your answers, the fuller the reports the Index will be able to submit to members.

1   (a)   What were your requirements from the course for which you engaged the services of the in-company training organisation?
    (b)   To what extent were these achieved?
    (c)   Was the course content what you required? If not, how did it differ?

---

2   (a)   Which were the best parts of the course?
    (b)   What made them so useful?

---

3   Were any parts of the course not up to standard? If so, please give details.

---

4   Were you satisfied with the way in which the organisation set about the training task – the lecturing personnel, methods of instruction, supporting paperwork, use of visual aids, etc?

---

5   . Would you use this training organisation for your in-company training purposes again?

I authorise you to make use of this report to such extent as you may think fit for the purpose of compiling records and other publications of the National Training Index, and to enter as my agent into such agreements with subscribers as you may consider necessary in order to protect me from any legal liability in respect of any inaccuracy or other defect in this report, whether arising through negligence or otherwise.

Signature   **Date**

Company/Organisation ....

Job Title ....

Figure 7.3 Minolta course appraisal form

MINOLTA

Course: ———————————————————————————————

Date: ———————————————————————————————

After completing this questionnaire, hand it to your trainer:

1. How would you describe the pace of the course?

    ☐ too slow

    ☐ about right

    ☐ too rushed

    Comments: ——————————————————————————

    ————————————————————————————————————

2. How would you describe the length of the course?

    ☐ too short

    ☐ about right

    ☐ too long

    Comments: ——————————————————————————

    ————————————————————————————————————

3. How clear and understandable was the course content?

    ☐ very clear and understandable

    ☐ clear and understandable

    ☐ not clear and understandable

    Comments: ——————————————————————————

    ————————————————————————————————————

4. How effective as the course in helping you learn the concepts and/or skills that were presented?

    ☐ very effective

    ☐ effective

    ☐ not effective

    Comments ——————————————————————————

    ————————————————————————————————————

Figure 7.3   Minolta course appraisal form – continued

5.   How valuable do you think the concepts and/or skills will be to you
     on the job?

☐   very valuable

☐   valuable

☐   not valuable

Comments: ─────────────────────────────────

───

6.   How enjoyable was the course?

☐   very enjoyable

☐   enjoyable

☐   not enjoyable

Comments: ─────────────────────────────────

───

7.   How would you rate this course in comparison with other sales
     training courses you have attended?

☐   better

☐   about the same

☐   worse

☐   not applicable

Comments: ─────────────────────────────────

───

8.   Now that you have completed the course, describe how you feel
     about it:-

☐   I'm glad I attended the course

☐   I'm not sure how I feel

☐   I wish I hadn't attended the course

Figure 7.3 Minolta course appraisal form – continued

9. Would you recommend the course to others in your organization?

☐ yes

☐ not sure

☐ no

If yes, to whom (i.e. title, level, background, years of experience, etc.)?

Comments: ───

───

10. If you have additional comments, please write them below:

───

───

───────────────────────────────────── ─

Figure 7.3   Minolta course appraisal form – concluded

Complete this section if asked by the trainer to do so.

Rate your trainer by checking a box beneath the response for each statement and providing any additional comments on the lines that follow.

The trainer:	Strongly Agree	Agree	Disagree	Strongly disagree
a. Had a thorough knowledge of the subject	☐	☐	☐	☐

Comments: ————————————————————————————————

| b. Created a comfortable and open learning environment | ☐ | ☐ | ☐ | ☐ |

Comments: ————————————————————————————————

| c. Seemed genuinely interested in whether or not I learned | ☐ | ☐ | ☐ | ☐ |

Comments: ————————————————————————————————

| d. Explained the purpose of each activity and provided clear directions | ☐ | ☐ | ☐ | ☐ |

Comments: ————————————————————————————————

| e. Provided, or asked participants to provide, useful answers to questions | ☐ | ☐ | ☐ | ☐ |

Comments: ————————————————————————————————

| f. Led productive and meaningful discussions | ☐ | ☐ | ☐ | ☐ |

Comments: ————————————————————————————————

| g. Helped me see the application of seminar concepts and/or skills to my job situation | ☐ | ☐ | ☐ | ☐ |

Comments: ————————————————————————————————

| h. Tied seminar segments together | ☐ | ☐ | ☐ | ☐ |

Comments: ————————————————————————————————

Figure 7.4 Cable and Wireless course assessment form

Cable and Wireless
Course Assessment Form

The aim of this form is to enable the Training Function of Corporate Personnel to gain information on the courses run within the company. This will allow us to assess the effectiveness of the training and shape the structure and content of future courses. We would be grateful if you could complete this form as fully as possible.

NAME: COURSE ATTENDED:

JOB TITLE: DATE(S):

DEPARTMENT: COURSE LOCATION:

REASON FOR ATTENDANCE:

Please give your opinion of the Course by grading the following points on a scale of 1 to 10.

1 = lowest level of satisfaction 10 = highest level of satisfaction

	Rating	Comments
1. Achievement of Course Objectives		
2. Coverage of Subject Matter		
3. Pre-Course Administration		
4. Supporting Arrangements (catering, accommodation, timekeeping etc.)		
5. Effectiveness of Presenter(s) Name:		
Name:		
Name:		
Name:		
Name:		
Name:		
Name:		
6. Overall Standard of Instruction		

Figure 7.4   Cable and Wireless course assessment form – concluded

7.   Did the Presenters use a variety of training tools (e.g. Audio Visual aids, O.H.P.'s etc.)?

8.   Did the Presenter(s) answer your questions and deal with your queries effectively?

9.   Which were the most useful parts of the course for you?

10.   How will you apply them in your present post?

11.   In which ways do you feel the programme could be improved?

12.   Would you recommend this programme to other colleagues within the group?

Any other comments (e.g. course structure, style and content, administrative arrangements etc.)

Signed:..   Date:..

Figure 7.5 Routledge, Chapman & Hall course/seminar/workshop appraisal form

Course/Seminar/Workshop Appraisal

Please complete within 5 days of attending the course and return to your departmental manager.

Course title:	
Course organisers:	
Date and duration:	Date: Duration:
Where was the course held?	
What was the main theme?	....
What were your objectives in attending the course?	....
List four major issues discussed:	....
Were your objectives achieved?	Rating: 1 2 3 4 5 6 7 8 9 10
Quality of speaker(s) *(Please rate each of the speakers separately)*	....

Were you given adequate opportunity to ask questions?   **Yes / No**

Would you recommend this course to colleagues?   **Yes / No**

Figure 7.5   Routledge, Chapman & Hall course/seminar/workshop appraisal
form – concluded

What proportion of the course was relevant to your needs?   ....%

Were there any topics which should have been included?
....
....
....
....
....
....
....

Summarize your overall impression:
....
....
....
....
....
....
....
....

Give two (or more) ideas which could be useful to you:
....
....
....
....
....
....
....

Did you gather any ideas/suggestions which could be implemented by this department or
Routledge generally?
....
....
....
....
....
....
....

Name: ....   Date: ....

Performance evaluation

Here the actual performance of the trainees is tested, again sometimes doing so before and after the event. Certain skills lend themselves to precise measurement. One can imagine an activity like typing skills being measured in just this way, with the words per minute recording the success, or otherwise, of the participants as a result of the training that had been going on. Other skills will only lend themselves to more subjective measurement, but there is no reason why this cannot be a reasonable guide.

Example

In our continuing example, managers could be rated – by both tutor and peers – using a checklist of some sort (see the example in Figure 7.6) – and this would be helpful in both an overall sense, and in highlighting specific areas that are either excellent, or remain poor.

Impact evaluation

Impact evaluation measures the effect of the training itself, and can therefore be carried out after any suitable period of time, since the training event has taken place. There is no reason why this should not be years later, or conducted in a way that makes no reference to the course that the trainer has in mind, though it will, more usually, be closer to the event.

In addition, it may even be valid to measure the change in supervisory skills, not by testing those who attended a course, but by testing those they manage. Similarly, there may be opportunities to read something about training effectiveness into organizational results in the longer term, though care is necessary here; there are normally already more than enough people ready to take the credit for successful results in any organization (and some who might welcome poor training as an excuse for poor results, given half a chance), and there will no doubt be influences other than training at work.

Whilst this is an area that must be approached with care, there is great merit in taking the longer term view, and comparatively few circumstances where this appears to be done.

In general, the moral is clear. Measure what your training is doing. Not just immediately; an appraisal form completed right at the end of the meeting will gain something from the euphoria of the moment – assuming there is some. But also seek a more considered view; this may well be different in nature, and no doubt more difficult to chase up once people are back to their various jobs.

Follow-up training

Training can do many things, certainly over time, and sometimes immediately. But, realistically, one training session, or one day, does not change the world. Follow-up is therefore often necessary. This may well take place, but not be

Figure 7.6 Presentation evaluation form

PRESENTATION EVALUATION FORM

PRESENTER:

TOPIC:

OBSERVER:

1 = good
4 = poor

BEGINNING ("Tell'em") – first impression	1	2	3	4	Comments:
Physical appearance					
Face/expression					
Voice/emphasis					
Stance					
Gestures					
Overall impression					

BEGINNING – introduction of topic	1	2	3	4	Comments:
Attention obtained					
Statement of intent					
Attitude displayed					
Rapport with group					
Interest					

Figure 7.6 Presentation evaluation form – concluded

MIDDLE ("Tell'em")	1	2	3	4	Comments:
Structured topic development					
Understandable					
Attractive					
Audience reaction anticipated					
Group in accord					
Attention built					
Maintains initial impression					
Overall impression					

END ("Tell'em")	1	2	3	4	Comments:
Topic round-up					
Summary of points made					
Audience acceptance conclusion/action					
End on high note					
OVERALL IMPRESSION					
IMPRESSION OF WHOLE PRESENTATION					

formal – on the job training with the line manager, perhaps. On other occasions it is not only formal, but an inherent part of the initial session. Whilst the on-going responsibility of the line manager can only be hinted at here, follow-up training that is an integral part of the whole is worth a few words. A number of approaches can be used to give this kind of continuity:

- 'part-work' programmes are, as the name suggests, in parts. Four evenings, perhaps, instead of two days. This may not only be useful when time is at a premium, but concentrates attention automatically over a longer period. If the four evenings are one per week, then attention continues, to some degree, for a whole month. There need to be logical breaks within the topics for this to work well, and this may not always be the case.
- 'sandwich' programmes are not only in two parts, one day followed by a second in a month or the like, they can be linked by a project of some sort.

We move towards the end, and come back to a premise stated at the outset; training is a continuous process. The trainer's job is never done.

Appendix: Ready-to-use training material

Once upon a time there were few ways to create training material. Research, poring over textbooks, was one. Experience, yours or someone else's, was another. And make no mistake, plagiarism is the trainer's stock-in-trade. In more recent years, plagiarism has been, in a sense, legitimized, and there is a growing amount of material in published form, ready to use.

Gower, the publishers of this book, can probably claim to have been the pioneers in this area of 'ready made' training sessions and exercises. Whilst they can now boast a considerable library of material, they are no longer the only producers of such material. It is, however, a sufficiently new phenomenon, and certainly a sufficiently useful one, to be worth a mention and an example.

Typically these resources are produced as a ring binder containing a series of exercises or workshop materials in looseleaf form. Although they cost more than a conventional book, they represent very good value for money. They take various forms: some designed to be followed slavishly, others to be the basis of some training activity to which the trainer adds to create the final unit. All draw on experience: they are tried and tested, and represent a useful shortcut to producing an original course from scratch.

As the author of a volume of this type (*20 Activities for Developing Sales Effectiveness*, written with Marek Gitlin for Gower), I cannot claim to be an entirely unbiased observer; though as a user of others, I would like to think that my comments were valid. Whatever else, my authorship allows me to reproduce here one 'activity' from my own volume; whilst perhaps not typical, it does give a good idea of what is available in this kind of format. The volume concerned is designed for sales training, but the topic selected, 'Handling complaints', is reasonably general (and most organizations have to cope with this occasionally).

The material is reproduced, reduced from the A4 page size in which it is published, without comment. Most volumes of this type grant some kind of waiver in the copyright restrictions on a purchaser, allowing, for instance, the copying of handouts for participants, or the production of overhead projector slides from the masters provided. A number of symbols are used in these publications: here you will see:

    Overhead transparency

    Handout sheet

A list of the Gower. publications of this sort appears at the end of this appendix (see page 125).

Extract from *20 Activities for Developing Sales Effectiveness*, P. Forsyth and M. Gitlin, Gower 1988.

5

Handling complaints

'I've got a bone to pick with you....'

All companies, even the best run, are likely to receive complaints. Some will be directed by letter or telephone to the sales office; others, by accident or design, could greet the salesman as he walks optimistically in to his customer's office.

As it is difficult to sell to a customer with a prior complaint, all complaints must be resolved. Handling complaints requires some planning and, above all, a calm approach.

This exercise will assist salesmen to reach satisfactory conclusions.

Aims

To emphasize why it is important to respond to complaints.
To review and practise approaches to do so effectively.

Time

Session length: 2 hours

Extract – continued

5.0-2

Resources

Lecture area with OHP, screen and flipchart.
Layout to facilitate discussion and role-playing.

Materials

Session Guide
5.1   Task sheet 1
5.2   Handout
5.3   OH transparency
5.4   Task sheet 2

Extract – continued

Session Guide

		Approx time
1	Introduce the Activity emphasizing the importance of (a) the need to resolve *all* complaints, (b) the dangers of ignoring any and (c) in-company procedures.	15 mins
2	Distribute task sheet 1 (5.1). Allow the participants ten minutes to complete the exercise. Review and discuss individual responses, at the same time compiling on the flipchart a composite list of complaints under each heading.	20 mins
3	Distribute and discuss the notes contained in handout 5.2. These are summarized on OHP (5.3).	30 mins
4	Role Play. Distribute task sheet 2 (5.4) to the participants.	30 mins
5	Conclude the session by selecting two or three recurring or difficult-to-resolve complaints (see the participants' responses to task sheet 5.1), and lead an open discussion on how to satisfactorily conclude each one.	30 mins

USER COMMENTS

Extract – continued

5.1-1

Handling Complaints: task sheet 1

Most complaints can be classified as complaints concerning:

The product	suitability; reliability; etc.
Service	delivery; installation; after-sales service
People	salesman, service engineers; sales support staff
Policies	sales terms and conditions; guarantees; administration and documentation
External factors	postal delays; traffic congestion; product design; availability of spares.

In each of the boxes below (a) list an example of a past or present complaint which *you* handled/are handling and (b) rate the degree of difficulty of resolving each.

Complaints

PRODUCT	SERVICE	PEOPLE	POLICY	EXTERNAL FACTOR

Extract – continued

5.1-2

Handling difficulty

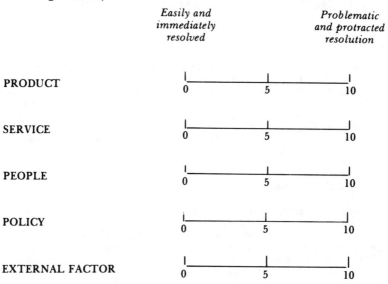

Easily and immediately resolved

Problematic and protracted resolution

PRODUCT

SERVICE

PEOPLE

POLICY

EXTERNAL FACTOR

Extract – continued

5.2-1

Handling Complaints: handout

Introduction

In a way, complaints should be welcomed. Consider what frequently happens when a customer does *not* complain. He stops using the product, relates a negative story to colleagues and friends, and becomes highly susceptible to competitors' overtures.

Thus, no complaint should be considered so minor as to be totally ignored. However *you* qualify a complaint, you must remember that to the customer, getting it resolved may be a key task in his day's plan of action.

Whether or not the customer remains loyal to your company and your product may turn on your ability to sympathetically deal with his complaint.

Types of Complaint

All complaints can be classified as 'justified' or 'unjustified'. However, these are terms which reflect *your* perspective: the customer's, irrespective of the facts of the case, may be different and continue to reflect the 'rightness' of his complaint even after your innocence in the matter is no longer in dispute.

This notion underscores the two elements present in many complaints: the practical element (the problem, the facts, the repercussions) and the emotive element (which can cloud the realities of the situation).

Dealing With Complaints

Of the two elements in a complaint, it is the emotive element which is frequently the driving force and, if not handled appropriately, can cause the most damage.

It is this point which supports the following method of handling complaints. The technique can be easily remembered by the word **LADDER**.

1 LISTEN: Listen not just at the beginning but throughout. *Let the customer express his emotions*, however hurtful or 'unjustified' these are. Listen carefully and make notes on the strategic issues at the core of his complaint.
2 ASK FOR HIS NAME: Get this as early on as possible, and also his title, his company and the location of the complaint, i.e. 'at our Birmingham branch', 'in our Number 2 plant', 'on production line 4'.
3 DETAILS: Ask for the precise nature of the problem, when it arose, how it arose and the people involved at the time.
4 DEVELOPMENTS: Get a complete run-down of the impact or repercussions of the problem. This is important. The customer may attribute lost revenue or costs to the problem and expect your company to reimburse him. You therefore need to know what liabilities you may be responsible for, *before* offering open promises of putting everything right.
5 EXAMPLE: Offer an example of what you can do to resolve the problem, hence answer the complaint. Wait for the customer's reaction. The example offered may not completely satisfy the customer, in which case he will most probably

Extract – continued

specify what he wants. This will give you an opportunity to further probe for
details of the complaint and determine to what extent the customer is seeking
emotional satisfaction, as well as satisfaction of the strategic issue.
   On the other hand, your offer may entirely satisfy the customer.
6 RESOLUTION: Summarize the discussion and confirm precisely what you
   intend to do.

   Throughout, you should bear in mind a number of rules:

(i)	Sympathize with the customer and reassure him that you understand,
(ii)	Never argue,
(iii)	Never directly contradict,
(iv)	Summarize and clarify,
(v)	Apologize (but do not unreservedly accept any blame until you fully understand the complaint details and developments),
(vi)	Avoid phrases such as 'you claim', or 'in your view'. These may be interpreted as your disbelief.

   Naturally, as an employee of your company you are its legal representative and
anything you say or promise must be honoured by your company. Therefore, if at
any time you are not sure how to resolve a complaint or what liabilities you can
accept on your company's behalf, tell your customer and seek your manager's
opinion. The you can re-contact your customer assured of your stand.

Documentation

Complaint Forms (5.2-3) are a useful source of customer research, particularly if
they are (a) circulated to all relevant departments, (b) analysed and (c) used to
stimulate action.
   A simple follow-up letter to the customer, confirming the details of the original
conversation, should be the rule rather than the exception.

Extract – continued

5.2-3

Example of Complaint Form

To: _____   Copies to: [ ] Production

_____   [ ] Area Manager

                                                   [ ] Representative

                                                   [ ] _____

Taken by: _____ Date: _____ Time: _____

Complainant's Name:_____ Position: _____

                 Company: _____

                 Address: _____

                           _____

                           _____

              Telephone Number: _____

Nature of complaint

_____

_____

_____

_____

_____

ACTION

Action taken: Action promised:

Follow-up action suggested:

Extract – continued

HANDLING COMPLAINTS

LADDER

1 LISTEN

2 ASK FOR CUSTOMER'S NAME

3 DETAILS OF THE PROBLEM

4 DEVELOPMENTS

5 EXAMPLE OF POSSIBLE
   RESOLUTION

6 RESOLUTION: WHAT YOU
     AGREE TO DO

Extract – concluded

5.4-1

Handling Complaints: task sheet 2

Work in pairs. Refer to your responses to task sheet 1 (5.1).
   One of you should play a customer and the other himself.
   The customer should express a complaint. Using LADDER as the structure of the complaint-handling technique, the salesman should respond and find a satisfactory resolution to the problem.

GOWER ACTIVITIES AND EXERCISES

Change: A collection of activities and exercises
50 Activities for Achieving Change
50 Activities for Developing Counselling Skills
50 Activities for Developing Management Skills Volumes 1–9
50 Activities for Interpersonal Skills Training
50 Activities for Managing Stress
50 Activities for Self-Development
50 Activities for Teambuilding
50 Activities for Unblocking Organizational Communication Volumes 1 & 2
50 Activities for Unblocking your Organization Volumes 1 & 2
50 Activities on Creativity and Problem Solving
50 Problem Solving Activities
A Manual of Management Training Exercises
Cross-Cultural Communication: A trainer's manual
20 Activities for Developing Sales Effectiveness
20 Training Workshops for Customer Care
20 Training Workshops for Developing Managerial Effectiveness Volumes 1 & 2
20 Training Workshops for Improving Management Performance
20 Training Workshops for Listening Skills

Full details of all these publications are available from:
Gower Publishing Co Ltd
Croft Road
Aldershot
Hampshire GU11 3HR
England.

Index

Problem Solving in Groups
Second Edition

Mike Robson

Modern scientific research has demonstrated that groups are likely to solve problems more effectively than individuals. As most of us knew already, two heads (or more) are better than one. In organizations it makes sense to harness the power of the group both to deal with problems already identified and to generate ideas for enhancing effectiveness by reducing costs, increasing productivity and the like.

In this revised and updated edition of his successful book, Mike Robson first introduces the concepts and methods involved. Then, after setting out the advantages of the group approach, he examines in detail each of the eight key problem solving techniques. The final part of the book explains how to present proposed solutions, how to evaluate results and how to ensure that the group process runs smoothly.

With its practical tone, its down-to-earth style and lively visuals, this is a book that will appeal strongly to managers and trainers looking for ways of improving their organization's and their department's performance.

Contents

Part I: Introduction • The benefits of group problem solving• Problem-solving groups • Part II: Problem-Solving Techniques • The problem-solving process • Brainstorming • Defining problems clearly • Analysing problems • Collecting data • Interpreting data • Finding solutions • Cost-benefit analysis • Part III: Following Through • Presenting solutions • Working together • Dealing with problems in the group • Index.

1993   176 pages   0 566 07415 X

A Gower Paperback

Assertiveness for Managers

Terry Gillen

Do you, asks Terry Gillen, want to be the kind of manager who:

- motivates his or her team to achieve their objectives?
- inspires loyalty in subordinates?
- has the respect of colleagues?
- is highly regarded by senior management?
- feels self-confident at work?

Today's business environment is changing dramatically – and so is our understanding of management effectiveness, especially when dealing with people. A major requirement of successful managers is personal credibility; it helps them motivate staff, work better with colleagues and impress their 'superiors'. Personal credibility depends on the way managers interact with other – where they do so assertively they naturally exhibit the characteristics we value in other people and which staff admire particularly in a manager.

Terry Gillen's practical book opens with an assertiveness profile to help you assess your own skills. In Part One the foundations of assertiveness theory are related to the workplace. Workout pages assist skill development.

Part Two is a ready reference of how to behave assertively in a range of typical managerial situations.

1994   257 pages   0 566 07613 6

A Gower Paperback

Techniques of Training

A Guide for Managers and Practitioners
Second Edition

Leslie Rae

When the first edition of this book appeared in 1983 it quickly established itself as a standard work. Since then many thousands of trainers and managers have benefited from the author's unrivalled experience as trainer, teacher, consultant, broadcaster, lecturer and writer which is distilled in this volume. The book is designed to fill the gap between, on the one hand, slim glossaries of training terms and, on the other, the lengthy and sometimes jargon-laden volumes covering a single technique. In it the author reviews the main methods and approaches currently used in training and development. He describes each one briefly, setting out its advantages and disadvantages and indicating - with examples and case studies - where its use is most appropriate. For this second edition the text has been radically revised and extended to reflect the many new developments in training. It examines the changing roles of both the training practitioner and the line manager, and pays increased attention to such topics as non-verbal communication, the use of games and exercises and the increasing emphasis on evaluation.

The first edition and the hardback of the second edition were published under the title **The Skills of Training.**

Contents

Introduction: Training in the 1990s • There is more to training than you think • The lecture • Self development • Training at work • Learning in groups • One-to-one interaction training • Human relations training - I • Human relations training - II • Feedback • Evaluation and validation • Training for training • Appendix: the occasional trainer's guide to resources • Index.

1993   304 pages   0 566 07432 X

A Gower Paperback